W9-BFV-387

A Personal Grief
&
A Reasonable Faith

A Personal Grief

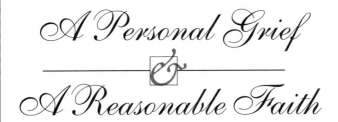

A Reasonable Faith

*A Mother's Journey from Tragedy to Triumph
in Understanding the Christian Faith*

NORMA E. SAWYERS

Dogwood Publishing
Flemington, Missouri
65650

Published by Dogwood Publishing
Box 80
Flemington, MO 65650

Printed in the United States of America

Scripture taken from the New American Standard Bible, © 1960, 1962, 1963, 1968, 1971, 1972, 1973, 1975, 1977 by The Lockman Foundation. Used by permission.

Verses marked (TLB) are taken from *The Living Bible* © 1971. Used by permission of Tyndale House Publishers, Inc., Wheaton, IL 60189. All rights reserved.

Scripture quotations marked (NIV) are taken from The Holy Bible, New International Version, Copyright © 1973, 1978, 1984 International Bible Society. Used by permission of Zondervan Publishing House. All rights reserved.

All excerpts by Francis A. Schaeffer taken from *The Complete Works of Francis A. Schaeffer* Vol I, Copyright 1982. Used with permission by Good News Publishers/Crossway Books, Wheaton, Illinois.

Library of Congress Catalog Card Number: 91-73415

Publisher's - Cataloging In Publication
(Prepared by Quality Books Inc.)

Sawyers, Norma Eileen, 1943-
        A personal grief and a reasonable faith : a mother's journey
        from tragedy to triumph in understanding the Christian faith /
        Norma E. Sawyers. — —
p.cm.
ISBN 0-9630031-0-0

1. Faith and reason. I. Title.

BT50   234.2

Dedicated to Karen

During her brief life, she was an inspiration to all who knew her. Her untimely death left a vacuum that can never be filled by earthly things or values. Only in the knowledge of God and by the love of Christ, our Lord, can such a great loss be understood and turned into victory!

Acknowledgements

I would like to express my deep appreciation to all the individuals who have been used by God to influence the writing of this book. I am particularly grateful to Carolyn Rogers for her assistance in preparing the manuscript. Without her special efforts, this book would not have been possible.

Contents

Foreword

Norma Sawyers has written a most delightful and important book for all who "seek the light." It is well written and I recommend it highly! In the author's "Introduction" to *A Personal Grief & A Reasonable Faith,* we are told: "This book is about the Christian concepts of 'faith' and 'reason, . . .'" and that this "relationship . . . is widely misunderstood by great numbers of contemporary Christians." As I tried to detail in my own book, *A Christian's Guide to Faith & Reason,* this current misunderstanding of faith and reason is without a doubt one of the most devastating to biblical Christianity.

This book is certainly about this most important and misunderstood topic, but it is about far more! For this book is the story of an intensely personal and painful journey by Norma Sawyers to an intelligent knowledge of God and to an understanding of (or faith in) the love and power of Jesus to make sense out of the senseless and to heal that which seems — by earthly standards — unable to be healed. Every seeker after truth, nonbeliever or Believer, will be touched by her personal story and helped by her journey to Christian faith! This is the wonderfully inspiring story of (and really the result of) an "ordinary" housewife's journey through a great personal tragedy to an understanding of "the Christian's need to know," necessary not just for herself but for every Believer. It will also challenge the nonbeliever to seek answers to the troubling questions which beset us all, to examine carefully the claims of Christianity.

Reading Mrs. Sawyers "A Personal Grief," (the biographical sketch at the beginning of this book) cannot help but touch you deeply. This sometimes tragic story will not only move you emotionally, but I believe you will be able to relate to her experience of grief, her sense (at times) of hopelessness, and her great desire for answers to life's most pressing questions. But as this story touches *you* so very deeply, it will also do something else for you. It will make you aware that *you* too have the obligation to seek out the answers to your questions and it will give you assurance that *you* — though yourself perhaps only an "ordinary" person — can find the answers! This fact in itself is cause for great rejoicing!

What makes this book truly unique is that Mrs. Sawyers is not a trained scholar, nor has she ever been to seminary, but this book is "living" proof that an "ordinary" person can use the thinking ability God gave every human being to seek and find intelligent answers to the difficult questions we all have, but to which very often we do not find ready answers in the world or — most unfortunately — in the church. Her personal tragedy moved Norma Sawyers to search for and find the inseparable connection between "faith" and "reason"; and, thereby to understand an essential part of the true essence of Christianity. Also, as a trained scholar myself, I should be quite blunt about the fact that just because Norma Sawyers is not a trained scholar in no way invalidates her scholarship or the importance of her material. In fact, just the opposite is true. The very fact that an "ordinary" person can search for the truth and find it should give us all great hope!

This does not mean, of course, that any of us can get by in not doing our "homework" for we simply cannot! By personal searching and study, by reading (among others) C. S. Lewis, unquestionably the greatest defender of the Christian faith in the twentieth century and perhaps in the last several, Norma Sawyers was brought into the light. Mrs. Sawyers says in her biographical sketch: "C. S. Lewis was the *first* Christian I had ever encountered who shared how he had 'thought through' or 'reasoned' his beliefs. Reading his books, I could see real answers did exist to problem questions about Christianity."

In my own life, I am currently debating the question which will soon become the book: *Does God Exist?: The Debate* (Harper and Row Publishers) with world famous atheist philosopher Antony G. N. Flew. During this debate Flew calls "for a systematic and progressive apologetic really beginning from the beginning: a rational apologetic, . . ." He is quite correct to issue this call. But as I write in the debate book: "this 'systematic and progressive apologetic, rational apologetic' [is] not coming in the near future . . . *not* because there is a lack of Christian scholars to produce this much needed joint effort, nor of the ability of such to be produced."

Most unfortunately, this effort is not coming exactly because of the reaction that Norma Sawyers and myself have come up against from more than one Christian publisher. In her attempt to get this book published, Mrs. Sawyers received a sincere and kind letter from one publisher which read in part:

After carefully looking at the material we have come to the conclusion that this is not a proposal that we should pursue for publication. . . . However, we did take careful look at your materials.

I want you to understand this does not necessarily imply that your material is unworthy of publication. In your particular case, the fact is that we have tried publishing similar kinds of books, but with little or no success. Our market simply does not seem to be interested in books defending the rationality of the Christian faith (emphasis added).

This Christian publisher shall forever remain nameless, known only to God (who weeps more than any of us over the folly of this statement) Norma and myself.

What a tragic statement — and tragic mistake — this Christian publisher has made. Do we allow the very ignorance which is the problem define the market? We must not! It is up to the Christian publishers to figure out a way to package — market — the needed product so effectively that the "sick" people will take their much needed "medicine," not to give up on the cure just because they have "tried" and found the patient reluctant to respond. The patient is not responding because: (1) Often they searched so long for answers and none were given by the church. (2) Many ministers and churches have accused them of being impious or disrespectful for even asking the questions (as was Norma Sawyers experience). (3) They themselves — the Christian publishers — have propagated the ignorance by so often offering such religious "fluff," so much consumer oriented garbage! Until this most tragic state of affairs is stopped, millions are being kept from the successful completion of their search. Books like this one, written by an "ordinary" person — not an academician — are of inestimable value in relating the fact that there is an answer and in introducing "ordinary" people to the answer!

This beautiful story reminds me of two scriptures: (1) "Ask, and it shall be given to you; seek, and you shall find; knock, and it shall be opened" (Matthew 7:7, Luke 11:9). This passage in Matthew's gospel goes on to say: "If you then, being evil, know how to give good gifts to your children, how much more shall your Father who is in heaven give what is good to those who ask Him!" (Matthew 7:11). And, (2) it reminds me of the many times I have stood in Keble College Chapel, the University of Oxford, and looked up at the beautiful painting "The Light of the World" by Holman Hunt. On the frame of that famous painting, at the bottom, is this scripture: "Behold, I stand at the door and knock; if anyone hears My voice and opens the door, I will come in to him, and dine with him, and he with Me" (Revelation 3:20). Norma Sawyers sought and found, knocked at the door and He opened it. But her discovery was the result of an intensely painful struggle and a long searching for answers to questions that had plagued her for years. Questions, I believe, that plague us all at one time or another!

This book is presented in the hope that, as this "ordinary" housewife saw and understood the light, other "ordinary" people will be moved to seek the light; and once it is found, to more fully understand and live their commitments to Christ. Every nonbeliever and Believer needs to come to this understanding and what better way to hear it than from one of their own! *A Personal Grief & A Reasonable Faith* is truly a story of a wonderful journey from tragedy to triumph in understanding and living the Christian faith! My prayer is that this book will inspire you to want to seek and understand the Truth, and to live it day by day! *Soli Deo Gloria (Glory to God alone)!*

— Terry L. Miethe, Ph.D., Ph.D.
Dean, Oxford Study Centre
Member, Christ Church [College], Oxford

Introduction

*T*his book is the result of a great personal tragedy, the death of my young daughter Karen, which exploded in my life into an intense search for a reasonable faith. The book begins with a biographical sketch, "A Personal Grief," which tells of my profound loss and of my resultant search for a reasonable belief; the main text, "A Reasonable Faith," is the consequence of that grief and of my search to find answers to questions I had (some from as early as my childhood) about God and ultimate reality.

Thus, this book is about the Christian concepts of "faith" and "reason." During the course of my painful struggle for spiritual answers, I became aware that the relationship of faith (belief) to reason (knowledge) is widely misunderstood by great numbers of contemporary Christians who seem to feel that knowledge is not as important as believing, or having faith. Viewing evangelism as a purely emotional process, rather than as a process necessitating intelligent knowledge both of God and of the world, they have forgotten the function of reason in conversion; and, also, in daily Christian living and loving.

The great Christian doctrines are not just claims of important moral teaching; they are inseparably linked to actual events of the past. If Christianity is true, it is because the Christian faith is founded on fact — real historical happenings as reported by the apostles. Chief among these is the resurrection of Jesus, the supreme fact of all history. Because Christianity claims to be objectively true, factual knowledge and historical evidence are important elements in distinguishing the truth claims of Christianity from other religions.

In a pluralistic world, an objective approach to the spreading of the Gospel is desperately needed, one that will give the non-Christian clear ground for actually trying Christianity. In *Faith Founded on Fact*, John Warwick Montgomery writes:

> *What is the non-Christian to do, when amid this din he hears the*

Christian message? Are we Christians so naive as to think that he will automatically, ex opere operato, accept Christianity as true and put away world-views contradicting it? And if we call out to him, "Just try Christianity and you will find that it proves itself experientially," do we really think that he will not at the same time hear precisely the same subjective-pragmatic appeal from numerous other quarters?[1]

Separating faith from reason, Christians are left with "individual opinion" which is merely subjectively or personally verifiable if that. Rendered defenseless to support their claims in relation to the great number of world religions claiming to be subjectively verifiable, about all such Christians can do to "defend" their faith is to say, "My religion is true for me." But adherents to opposing religions will also say, "Mine is true for me, so why should I accept your Christianity?"

Non-Christians need solid reasons for making a commitment to the Christian faith. Rather than expecting these people to accept the Christian message merely on the basis of our personal experience, believers should support important Christian claims to truth by the knowledgeable evidence of reason. Montgomery goes on to say:

Absolute proof of the truth of Christ's claims is available only in personal relationship with Him, but contemporary man has every right to expect us to offer solid reasons for making such a total commitment. The apologetic task is justified not as a rational substitute for faith, but as a ground for faith; not as a replacement for the Spirit's working, but as a means by which the objective truth of God's Word can be made clear so that men will heed it as the vehicle of the Spirit who convicts the world through its message.[2]

Paul Little, in *Know Why You Believe*, states, "our personal subjective experience is based on objective historical fact."[3] What matters is not how *much* faith we have, but the object in which we have placed our faith. Faith must be based on good reasons.

Unfortunately, twentieth century Christians have been widely exposed to the idea that reason is not important in bringing about conversions. Failing to understand the important role of knowledge in implanting faith, many contemporary Christians deny that argument or reason can lead to or away from belief. Clark Pinnock, in *Set Fourth Your Case*, observes:

People are constantly affected in their actions and choices by argu-

ments, intelligent or otherwise. The notion that nobody is ever converted to Christ by argument is a foolish platitude. It would be more accurate to say that the reason so few people are being converted to Him now is that so many Christians believe the fallacy. It is high time for us to restock the arsenal of Christian evidences and confront our contemporaries with a solid message.[4]

Pinnock stresses that the modern church desperately needs to reexamine its approach to evangelism. There is urgent need for "a new reformation in truth for the church".[5] Churches were intended, in part, to be intermediaries in bringing God and mankind closer together. If our churches are failing to perform this function, they should change or reform their evangelistic methods in order to adequately serve the spiritual requirements of the people.

In the sixteenth century, the Christian Reformation brought about badly needed reforms of the church; it is common knowledge that the Reformation and the Counter-Reformation that followed purified and strengthened both the Reformers and the Roman Catholic Churches. In a similar way, Pinnock and others believe the modern church could benefit from some drastic changes in its approach to evangelism. Many — though obviously not enough — modern church leaders emphasize that authentic Christian evangelism must involve the intelligent use of reason. John Shelby Spong, an Episcopal bishop, writes:

I am convinced that the only authentic defense of the faith involves honest scholarship, not anti-intellectual hiding from truth. There is a sense in which our scholarship ought to be so deep, so honest, and so intensive that the result will be either that what we believe will crumble before our eyes, incapable of being sustained, or that we will discover a power and a reality so true that our commitment will be total. If we do not risk the former we will never discover the latter. Nothing less than this seems worthy of Christians.[6]

In light of the serious need for change in the church today, the time is right for a book that examines the relationships of faith and reason to Christian evangelism and responsible Christian living. Christians need to become aware that a clearly reasoned presentation of the gospel is necessary to many people for conversion and to all Christians so they can mature in the faith.

Although I write from the perspective of an ordinary lay Christian with a deep, personal interest in the relationship of faith and reason and not from the viewpoint of a scholar holding numerous degrees, I have researched the subject of this book extensively. Suggestions for additional reading are provided at the close of this book for those who should wish to further examine this important topic.

A
Personal
Grief

David and Karen Sawyers
at ages 7 and 6

1

A Hint of Sorrow

It was Christmas 1981. A festive mood filled the atmosphere of our modest farm house as my loved ones and I gathered about our glittering Christmas tree surrounded by gaily wrapped presents. I glanced at my husband, Lewis, whom I had loved at first sight almost twenty years before. He was as handsome as ever with his dark hair streaked at the temples, his skin still firm on his muscular frame. He was as dear to me now as he had ever been. My eyes moved to our good-looking children, David and Karen, sixteen and fifteen, as they happily opened their gifts. Lewis and I were so proud of them — with their strong, young bodies and intelligent minds.

Suddenly, as I watched our children tearing paper from their packages, the air around me became kaleidoscopic with memories dancing merrily about like the tinsel reflections on our glittering tree. My thoughts retreated sixteen years to a Christmas long ago and to a baby boy, soft as silk, snuggled against my breast, his small body bathed in the warm light of our twinkling tree. Time moved onward another year to the gurgle of laughter as the baby boy, now a toddler, "hid" from me behind a similar Christmas tree while I rocked his newborn baby sister to sleep, her tiny head reposing peacefully upon my shoulder. Year by year, the remembrances passed in memory's eye. Two little tots with stars in their eyes opened presents on early Christmas morns. Squeals of delight were heard as velvety stuffed animals and brightly-colored pull toys were clutched to their small chests. As the years flashed by, a parade of dolls, trains, trucks, and games marched before my recollection until suddenly the small tykes had changed into splendid teenagers.

Abruptly returning to the present, I felt a familiar surge of gratefulness for my wonderful family. In bygone days I had often felt a wonder that

Lewis and I had been blessed with our beautiful children. Now, once again, my gaze fell upon David, his fawn-colored hair shining in the luminous glow of the tree, and upon Karen, her light hair catching the nuance of colors from the flickering bulbs. I could hardly believe our good fortune.

We were carefree that Christmas Day in 1981, not realizing that soon our circumstances would change. The next week passed normally until one cold evening when we all sat gathered around our television set. It was a tradition at our home to watch football during the holiday season, and this winter was no exception. Father and son had been continually engrossed that week in watching the sport, but Karen and I were bored.

Turning to me, she sighed, "Mom, do you want to go into the bedroom and read to one another while they watch football?"

I replied, "That's an excellent idea."

From the time David and Karen were small, they had always enjoyed having me read to them. Reading was the source of many of our best times. Over the years I had read story after story to my children, but now we had graduated to reading to each other.

Gathering up several issues of *Reader's Digest,* my daughter and I snuggled under the covers to read to one another. After reading several articles, we came to a story which touched our hearts deeply. We were both so overcome with emotion that we had to take turns reading.

At the time we had no way of knowing that the narrative we had just read would indirectly affect our lives forever. The written account was not only a hint of sorrow which would soon enter our lives, but also an instrument which God would later use in a remarkable way to change my entire life.

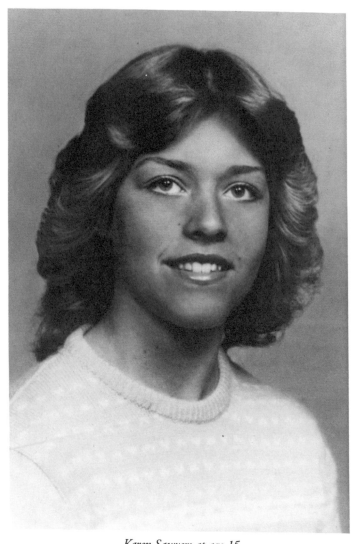

Karen Sawyers at age 15

2

Tragedy

*M*arch 4, 1982 — the day before our daughter's tragic accident — is etched in my mind forever. I have relived that day and those following it a thousand times.

Usually an outgoing person, there were times when Karen could be introverted. Both aspects of her personality were evident the day before her accident. On that afternoon Karen was particularly quiet — she came in after school, pulled up a stool, and watched television while I finished my work. My daughter seemed to have something on her mind. Later that evening the outgoing aspect of her personality was evident as she and David wrestled around playing "horse" after supper.

Karen always had a good sense of humor. That night as I was doing dishes, I asked her to come dry them for me. She replied, "Oh, Mom, I can't. I've got a broken leg!" Then she hopped into the kitchen on one leg as if the other were broken.

After my family went to bed that Thursday night, I thumbed through a seed catalog making plans for planting a garden later in the spring. Plans were also running through my mind concerning a spring house cleaning project for the weekend. I had no idea that my happy plans would soon change.

Tragedy struck on Friday, March 5, 1982. Finishing with my last customer at work, I glanced up at the clock to notice it was 3:05 p.m. The busy week was almost over, and my attitude was cheerful as I contemplated the weekend. As I was handing change to the customer, a young high school boy came running into the shop flinging his arms around aimlessly.

I wondered, *What is wrong with that boy?* He was so overcome with emotion he was speechless, but finally regained his composure suffi-

ciently to tell me Karen had been involved in an accident. At the same
time, another friend of Karen's had gone next door to tell Lewis. Immediately, my husband and I started sprinting toward the scene of the
accident one block away. As I ran, I reasoned that the boy's urgency was
undue alarm. I told myself repeatedly that the accident was probably a
minor mishap; surely it was nothing serious.

When we arrived at the scene, someone tried to restrain me, but I
pulled away — I had to see about my daughter. Horrified, I saw her
lying unconscious on the street, her eyes fixed and staring. People familiar with first aid were administering cardiopulmonary resuscitation.
Glancing at Lewis, I saw terror registered on his drawn face. My husband
began crying and moaning, "She's gone! She's gone!"

I don't believe it, I thought. *It's not true! Karen would be all right. My
daughter and I were fighters. I would stay by her side until she recovered.
She would be all right.* In a stupor from the shock of Karen's situation, I
watched as she continued to receive first aid. *This is unreal,* I kept
thinking. *Any moment now I will wake up and find this to be a bad dream.*

In hushed silence a large group of bystanders — friends and relatives
— gathered all around us. David was standing with his head leaned
against a parked truck; our son had walked up on the scene of his sister's
accident. Lewis was standing alone, his body wracked by sobs of grief.
My heart reached out to them. But I was numb, too numb to cry. Fear,
frustration, disbelief, grief, shock — these emotions now belonged to
our family and to our friends.

But how had this calamitous accident happened? Earlier our daughter
had decided to cut a school friend's hair. The two were riding the boy's
motorcycle on their way from school when a feed truck hit them at an
intersection. The force of the collision threw both riders toward a car
waiting at a stop sign. Karen was thrown under the car, her helmet came
off, and her head struck the pavement. Fortunately for the boy, his
helmet remained intact as he was thrown from the motorcycle into the
right rear tire of the car. He suffered a severe concussion and multiple
fractures but later recovered completely.

As we waited for the ambulance to arrive, time seemed to stand still.
Trembling with fear for Karen, I wondered, *What is taking them so long?
Don't they know my daughter could be dying?* Finally, the wailing ambu-
lance rushed up to the scene. After examining Karen's condition, the

medical attendants decided to transport our daughter to a small, nearby hospital to stabilize her condition. Numb with panic, I accompanied my daughter on the trip. Lewis and David took our car as we all headed for the medical facility. Again and again, I tried to convince myself that Karen was going to be all right. Yet I felt so frightened. My mouth became so dry that my tongue felt like cotton. I watched as the paramedic worked with my daughter in the ambulance. *Just keep at it,* I thought to myself. *Keep working with her. She'll come through.*

Although the ride to the hospital seemed to take forever, at last we sped into the hospital emergency entrance. Breathing heavily, I followed the attendants as they rushed Karen into the building. A feeling of intense fear swept over me as I watched my daughter disappear into the emergency room. Suddenly, I felt that I had to sit down. After a period of time, a doctor came to inform us that Karen's condition was critical. Feeling certain the physicians at a larger hospital would have a better prognosis, I told myself this doctor was mistaken.

After waiting for some time, we were taken to the hospital chapel. I thought we had been taken there to pray for Karen, but Lewis was afraid we were in the chapel to learn she had died. A nurse started to tell us something about our daughter but was interrupted by a doctor who informed us that Karen was to be transferred to larger hospital facilities. Watching as they reloaded our daughter for the trip, we were told by the ambulance attendants that I couldn't ride with Karen this time. We followed the ambulance in our car until mechanical problems forced us to finish our trip with relatives. Everything was going wrong.

The ride seemed endless. Karen was in the ambulance, and we had no idea what was happening — we didn't even know if she was still alive. Lewis' brother and sister-in-law tried to comfort us during the trip by talking. Lewis, David, and I sat silently in the back seat. Our thoughts and our feelings could not fit into words.

Arriving at the large hospital, we were taken to a room to wait for the doctor's report. A short time later a physician came to give us a prognosis on Karen. She was in a deep coma from the severe head injury, not breathing on her own, and unresponsive to all stimuli — she was "clinically silent." Electroencephalograms had been taken, and they were flat. More head scans would be performed later to see if there was any change, but the outlook wasn't good. We were informed that our daughter's life was being temporarily sustained by the assistance of machines. Drugs administered through the vein were keeping her heart beating and maintaining her blood pressure, and a respirator was pumping oxygen into her lungs.

Although the doctor was trying to gently tell us Karen's condition was terminal, I could not accept what he was saying. With my ears I listened to him speaking the words, but with my heart I could not hear him. Staring at me strangely, the doctor asked, "Do you understand what I am saying, Mrs. Sawyers?" Although I could hear myself answering, "Yes," I found it hard to believe I was actually speaking. How could I utter a word that signified the collapse of our world?

Taken to another waiting room near Intensive Care, we continued the unbearable waiting. Many of Karen's friends joined us at the hospital to await news of her condition; we were glad they were there for support. That evening and the following days were a blur of faces and of embraces as our family and our friends sought to comfort us.

As we waited for visiting in ICU, many questions came to torture me: Why had this senseless calamity befallen *our* little one? Why did it have to be Karen? It wasn't fair! Karen was so beautiful, her life so full of hope and of promise. Was life being stolen from her just as she was beginning to blossom and to taste life's joys?

The three of us were finally allowed into Intensive Care to see Karen. My daughter's chest moved up and down as the mechanical respirator breathed for her. She was comatose and made no spontaneous movements; her eyes were partially open and staring. A nurse explained that everything possible was being done for our daughter. I looked down upon my precious daughter's motionless body. Taking her hand, I softly spoke to her, "I love you, Karen, We all love you." We all spoke loving words as if she were listening. There was no response as Karen continued to lie still and seemingly lifeless. She appeared withdrawn from life.

Day and night merged into a blur as we continued our sad vigil. Questions concerning my daughter filled me with mental anguish: Does she know anything that is going on? What if she is suffering and can't tell me. Despair swept over me. Oh, how could our family bear this torment? Longing to escape the mental torture, I wished to be home so I could just run down the road and scream. Would it help to be able to do that? Where was my help? What was my help?

As we continued to wait, my thoughts retreated to the previous Christmas holidays to the night when Karen and I had decided to read to one another while the men watched football on television. Snuggled under the covers, we read several articles before coming to the condensed version of the book, *Song for Sarah,* a series of letters written by Paula D'Arcy for her daughter, Sarah. Mrs. D'Arcy began her letters in 1973 when she learned that she was pregnant with her daughter. She writes, "I little guessed then that within two and a half years they [the letters] would be my detailed recollection of a time and a life that were suddenly and unkindly ended."[1] Mrs. D'Arcy's husband and small daughter were later killed in a tragic accident.

Thinking back to the time when Karen and I had read the account, I remembered telling her I didn't think I could bear it if a tragedy like that ever happened to us. Karen had said, "Mom, you would have to." Only a little over two months has passed since our reading of the account of Mrs. D'Arcy's sorrow. Now, a similar misfortune was happening to my own family. In the midst of my grief, there was no way I could know that God was planning to use the D'Arcy article in another way in my life — that in the future God would use the same article to direct me to a man who would be a witness to me in the dark night of my soul.

On Saturday we conferred again with the neurologist. "I'm sorry to have to tell you that the EEG shows no improvement," he said. "The readings are flat. Another brain scan will be taken tomorrow to see if there is any change. If there is no change, after the period of time required by law, your daughter should be taken off the machines maintaining life functions. To leave her on the life-supporting machines would only prolong her present condition artificially. Medically we have done all we can. We don't expect you to make the decision — after the prescribed period of time has passed, we will decide."

My emotions screamed inside me. How could physicians talk that way? The basic, precise medical terminology was necessary to clarify the situation, but it all seemed so impersonal. He was talking about my daughter, my little girl, who had laughed and loved only hours before. Now, she was in a coma, her languid body motionless as the doctors decided what to do. But I couldn't fault the physicians; I knew they cared despite their medical terms.

By Saturday night we were totally exhausted. We had not slept since our daughter's accident and still wore the same clothes. Clothing, however, was the last thing on our minds as we thought of the sad misfortune which had befallen our daughter and as we waited for visiting to be permitted in ICU. That night, lounging in the waiting room, we did manage a little fitful sleep. Often during that long night, I awoke to go through all the "if-onlys": If-only we had told Karen that she couldn't cut the boy's hair; if-only we had told her not to ride on the boy's motorcycle; if-only we could turn back the clock and make this stop; if-only. . . .

We had always been so careful with our children, never taking chances on their health or on their safety. When they were sick, we immediately took them to the doctor. Once David had broken his foot, and Karen had hurt her knee in sports. We took both to specialists where they received the finest care. Now, after all the years of care and concern, this horrible tragedy had happened to our daughter.

Two days had passed since our daughter's tragic accident. It was Sunday morning, March 7, 1982. It was so hard to live. I didn't know how my mind could tolerate the unbearable shock of our little girl's situation. That morning Karen's physicians had informed us there was no hope for her recovery. It was apparent to them that our daughter's brain had been irreversibly damaged. Karen had lost her higher brain functions — she could no longer think, no longer feel. In other words, Karen was no longer Karen. And, the doctors said, Karen never would be again.

Medically, our daughter was only existing. We knew Karen wouldn't want such a condition to continue. The fiesty, fun-loving girl we had known and loved for fifteen years would not want any part of that sort of helpless existence. For Karen's sake the doctors felt that the best thing to do was to cease artificial life-support. Further treatment was hopeless. We had to let go of our Karen; we had to let our beloved daughter die in peace.

David Sawyers at age 23

3

Profound Grief

$\mathcal{A}$s I awoke the following morning, the realization washed over me like a tidal wave that my daughter was gone. My inner-most being felt despair as waves of sorrow engulfed me. From that moment each new day meant facing the paradox of the unfaceable, awakening each morning to the reality of what had happened to Karen. Across the bed and in the next room, I knew my husband and my son were experiencing their own profound grief.

Our house screamed of Karen's absence. The void was almost palpable, the air thick with sorrow and with uncertainty. From the moment we first arrived home from the hospital after Karen's death, we didn't know how to handle our grief. We were hurting so badly. How could we go on living and breathing with all this hurt?

It seemed that the world should stop, but I knew it wouldn't. While I felt incapable of going on with life, the rest of the world was moving on as usual. People everywhere were enjoying their everyday lives, but our world was upside down. As we drove to the funeral home to make final arrangements, vehicles such as garbage and milk trucks whizzed up and down the road, reminding us that life was continuing.

Sadly, we made the preparations for our daughter's funeral. With great care we planned each detail. We had originally intended to keep the casket closed, but the funeral director felt this would be a mistake. Perhaps he thought others needed to be reminded that Karen was no longer in her body, that she had said good-by to earth. Although this was a struggle for me, we followed his suggestion. It was difficult because I had wanted to preserve Karen's former identity, to preserve the memory of the way she looked before she died. Somehow, it seemed a violation for everyone to be staring at our daughter's body in death. I have since learned that many ministers feel that a closed casket is better.

On Tuesday, March 9, 1982, with broken hearts, we buried our dear daughter. No words can express the inward misery we felt.

In the sorrowful days following Karen's death, it was not easy for me to see things realistically. Wasn't there some way to bend events to make this stop? Couldn't things be reversed somehow to restore the past? If only this were just a nightmare that would soon end. But it wasn't a bad dream; it was reality — Karen was gone. What a terrible finality! Everything seemed futile and hopeless. There was no answer — no way of straightening it out.

I missed Karen. I wanted to see my daughter, to put my arms around her, to hold her near. Sometimes, longing for her presence, I went into her room and hugged one of her sweaters close; there was nothing else I could do.

I was nearly paralyzed by my grief — it took an extreme effort of will for me to function even at the simplest level. My legs dragged as I mechanically went through the motions of cooking, cleaning, and laundry washing. Shakily, I proceeded through each task, summoning up just enough energy to do the chores which just had to be done.

Seriously considering withdrawing from society and hiding at home, I dreaded having to face people all day at my job. Yet I knew that contact with others would compel me to cope with life at least on a surface level. If I stayed home, I had no idea what might happen. So, two weeks after my daughter's death, I returned to work at my shop. Apprehension filled me each day as I thought of facing my tasks. I didn't know how I could perform duties at the shop because I had so much trouble concentrating. From the moment I had seen Karen lying unconscious on the street after the accident, I had suffered from a sensation similar to a stupor. This vacant sensation stayed with me for months. As daily affairs occurred around me, it was difficult for me to tune in or to communicate.

My customers went our of their way to offer me sympathy; I couldn't have survived at work if they had not been understanding. Nevertheless, it was difficult for me to appear interested and attentive in what was going on around me. As customers chatted with me, I hoped I was nodding at the correct times and saying the right things. I was too preoccupied to be good company. By the end of each day, I was exhausted from the struggle to maintain a pretense of alertness.

Struggling with a barrage of emotions — grief, anger, frustration, confusion, bitterness — I found it difficult to be alert to everyday affairs. Feeling bitter toward Karen's physicians, I wondered if they had really told us the truth about her condition. Why couldn't they have done something to help her? After all, weren't doctors miracle workers? What went wrong? Did we make a mistake in believing them? Months later, when I was thinking more clearly, I realized that Karen's physicians had not been trying to deceive us. After reading a book which thoroughly explained how doctors determine the extent of brain damage after injuries, I understood that my daughter's physicians had done the right thing in removing her life support systems.

I also blamed myself for Karen's absence. Her death went against the most basic of my parental instincts. After all, a mother's first task is to preserve the safety of her child. It seemed my fault that Karen had died because I was responsible for her as a parent. Yet, I couldn't save her. It was months before I could see that these were irrational thoughts, that I was blaming myself needlessly.

And, I felt bitter toward God — if there was a God. I wondered how I could know if God existed. What kind of a Creator would allow a beautiful, intelligent, fifteen-year-old girl to die in such a tragic way? This wasn't fair at all! I couldn't think of another girl any prettier or sweeter than Karen. She had so much potential. As I thought of my daughter's hopes and plans for the future, my heart overflowed with grief and with anger. If there was a God, why didn't he allow Karen to go on with her life? It all seemed so cruel and so unjust. Surely there was more to this than seemed to meet the eye, but if so, where were the answers? Would the Bible help me? If I searched the Bible, would I really be able to find out why this tragedy had happened to Karen?

On the other hand, if there was no God, life was purposeless. What was the reason for living if this tragic world was all there was to our existence? Entangled in a seemingly hopeless quandary, I was desperately searching for answers to the perplexing religious questions which were troubling me. I didn't know how I could continue to live with the unbearable uncertainty. Somewhere I had to find answers.

For even a moment, I couldn't seem to escape from my sorrow or from my confusion. The normal, healthy "escapes" which I had relied on all my life were suddenly stolen from me. I found it impossible to become absorbed in a book or in television because my attention span had become so short. Feeling disassociated from my surroundings and from the concerns of the world, I found it difficult to carry on an ordinary conversation. Little details of life now seemed so insipid. In fact, nothing really seemed very important anymore. It was difficult to show interest in hearing about someone's Tupperware party or the latest gossip because I simply didn't care. I realized, however, that I needed to feign interest in the things going on around me for the sake of others. Food no longer attracted me because now my appetite was gone; it was difficult for me to even consume an entire sandwich. While other people were on diets, I was losing weight without even trying. Sleep wasn't an escape either. Dozing off to sleep at night, I intermittently woke up with a start, with an empty feeling in the pit of my stomach. Night and day, the realization of the loss of my daughter weighed heavily on my mind.

Sometimes I panicked. What if the quicksand of my grief pulled me farther and farther down until I lost my mind? In the first months after Karen's death, I visited three different psychiatrists in my search for help. They didn't provide much, except to alleviate my fears that I was going insane. Each told me that I was going through the normal grief process which is very slow for parents who have lost a child. One of them, sensing I was searching for spiritual as well as emotional help, asked if I would be interested in talking with the minister of a large church in the same city. Of course, I was interested, so he made the appointment me.

Later, I drove back to the city to talk with the well-known pastor about the deep, philosophical questions which had been troubling me. Although he was a very kind and sympathetic person, he tended to be noncommittal on the questions which were bothering me the most. For example, concerning the question of my daughter's eternal status, he assured me that she was safe with God, but he wouldn't explain his reasons for the statement. I felt he was merely trying to console me rather than give me thorough answers. I was back where I had started. Wasn't there anyone who would answer my questions?

Karen's death had unbalanced all the relationships of our lives within our immediate family and with all the people who were important in our lives. Her grandparents not only had the loss of a grandchild to bear but also had to witness our grieving. For my parents, especially, the loss was so great — Karen was their only granddaughter. I felt such sadness for them.

The patterns of our life together did not work anymore; everything was out of kilter. Karen was, we had believed, to have filled a place in our lives until the end of our days. Now, that space was empty. She would have grown up, become an adult, perhaps married and had children of her own. But she would still have been a part of our lives — until *we* died. It seem an affront — a reversal of nature — that she had died before us.

As a family we each carried our mourning in an individual way; the stages of our grief and the expressions of our sorrow were different. Grasping the reality of the situation, Lewis and David cried more in the initial weeks following Karen's death. In contrast, I experienced a numb first stage of grief in which I was too stunned to cry. Later, reading books on the subject of grief, I learned that the mind often shields and protects itself from traumatic shock until the psyche can adjust and accept the reality.[2] This explained why it was months before my tears finally flowed, before my mind could accept the reality of my loss. It seemed then that I'd never stop crying.

After the first few months, we talked very little about Karen's death or about the effect it had on us. Our emotions were hidden inside. I felt a need to communicate, but Lewis and David could not talk of Karen easily; they hurt too deeply. Not wanting to alienate my own family, I tried to refrain from broaching the subject.

Lewis ached terribly but his experience of Karen's loss was different from mine. I needed to remember her life, to look at her pictures and physical articles. This was not helpful for Lewis; the pain grew worse when he remembered. My husband spent almost every minute of his time working because keeping busy seemed to be a source of help for him.

David went on about his business, but I knew that deep inside he was suffering. I realized that the emptiness David was experiencing was unfathomable; what a lesson to learn at only sixteen. To be young and to be faced with the enormity of his loss was awesome. I longed to comfort my son, but what could I possibly say to David that would help to ease the pain and the sorrow of the loss of his sister?

Many other people missed Karen as well. The most poignant reminder of this came over one year after her death. Lewis and I were babysitting for young friends of ours, Kenny and Debbie McShane, while they attended her father's funeral. When Karen was alive, she had frequently babysat for the McShane's small boys, Troy and Tyler. She loved both boys but was especially captivated by Tyler, the youngest. The day we babysat with the boys, Tyler asked me to read to him and followed me into Karen's room to help get the books which were in a bottom dresser drawer. Tyler was only about one year and nine months old when Karen was killed, and I didn't think that he still remembered her. But as Tyler and I walked into Karen's room, he turned to me and said sadly, "Karen's gone." Surprised that he still remembered her, I asked gently, "Do you miss Karen?" Tyler answered, "I miss Karen."

Lewis and Norma Sawyers

4

One Sweet Day

A friend of ours who lost a son in 1979 sent us the book, *The Bereaved Parent*, by Harriet Sarnoff Schiff. Books of this type, and association with other parents who had also lost children, were my biggest emotional help. We began attending meetings for bereaved parents, and this also provided support for a time. When a person is hurting, he needs others who understand just what it is that he is experiencing. Healing balm is contained in the sincerely spoken words: "I know exactly how you feel." I soon recognized that I was craving something more than just emotional help, however. I was hungry for spiritual guidance.

It continued to be difficult for me to function at everyday tasks while searching for seemingly unobtainable answers about life: Why did this terrible tragedy happen to my daughter? How did God fit into the picture? Was there really a God who cared? Anxiety over profound questions of this type tore at my soul night and day. Few moments of consciousness existed for me that my mind was not churning these uncertainties over and over. Wrestling with the unresolved philosophical questions, I read the entire New Testament except for Revelation and studied parts of the Old Testament. In my search for religious truth, I was unable to find real answers on my own, however. Spiritually starving, I was desperate for genuine guidance.

I had been struggling with unanswered religious questions for most of my life. Until I reached about seven years of age, however, my life was fairly normal. My parents loved me and were able to give me a sense of security. Only vague memories remain of the times I attended church with my family at this tender age, but I do faintly remember the solemn atmosphere of the church as the congregations listened attentively to the sermons.

Although everything appeared to be running smoothly in our lives at this time, underneath it all I sensed that something was terribly wrong; my mother seemed so nervous. Often she would sit for hours exploring the Bible and crying softly. Looking back, I wonder what mother was seeking in her Bible. Did she find solutions to the problems which were troubling her?

My mother later suffered a nervous breakdown. Although other factors may have contributed to mother's illness, the tragic death of her father by suicide when she was only a young girl may have started her difficulties. The shock of his death had been devastating; the tragedy had pressed on her mind for years. Mother needed someone to minister to her at a time of deep grief and confusion. When mother required help the most, however, she discovered that many people were ashamed of the mental problems which had caused her father's suicide. There were no reassuring words to soothe my young mother's emotional and spiritual wounds.

While mother was recuperating in a mental institution, I lived off and on with my maternal grandmother for about a year. Frequently, my father and I visited mother at the hospital. I distinctly remember the first time we went to see her. The wind, whistling through cracks beside windows in the waiting room, made a mournful noise which was the most sorrowful sound I have ever heard. Even today, hearing that same sound, my thoughts return to that long ago time and to the sadness I felt in my heart.

Mother suffered two breakdowns. During her second hospitalization, I stayed home with father. Happily, when this special lady came home from the hospital the second time, her illness had been cured. She never returned to the institution again.

We attended church only once after mother came home from the hospital. Participating in a Sunday School class discussion, mother added a comment. One insensitive person replied, "Don't pay attention to her; she has been in a mental institution." As a family this was the last time we attended church together. I often wondered why my parents no longer attended church. Only recently did I discover this snide remark was the reason. I can understand now why mother couldn't bring herself to go back. It makes me wonder if individuals who make such thoughtless statements realize the impact their words can have on other lives.

Mother faced many difficulties after her hospitalization; in those days a terrible stigma was placed on people who had suffered mental illness. Many people were embarrassed that mother was having "trouble." Her condition was considered a weakness or something wished upon herself instead of a real illness. Most people didn't realize that chemical imbalances and other biological problems could cause the difficulties. Strangely, physical ailments were met with real sympathy, but emotional problems were very often met with scorn.

Mother was a very capable person with many hidden talents, but society constantly reminded her that she had spent time in an institution. Every time my poor mother fumbled, someone was quick to bring up a reason. "Oh, you know she has had two nervous breakdowns," they wagged their tongues. "You'll have to overlook her." Because of heavy sedation, mother could not remember several incidents which happened during her breakdown. Sometimes she was unable to remember past events. "Oh, it's her nervous breakdown," the diatribe continued. Few people showed my mother the trust and the respect she deserved. I felt sad.

Church going for me was confined to Vacation Bible School in the summers and to a few trips with neighbor children. Many questions about Christianity remained in my mind, but the real puzzlers were never solved. Attending church, I felt confused. If I couldn't find answers there, where could I find them? I couldn't make a decision about Christianity if my questions remained unanswered. Yet, I longed to discover the meaning of my existence.

The years passed by; I became a teenager. But still I was confused about life, about God. Who was he? Was he the God of the Christians or of some other religion? How could I know for sure? There was no one with whom I could talk about my questions. It didn't help to attend church — there I was told to have faith, not to ask questions. Questioning was considered impertinent or lacking reverence for God. Anyone who questioned faced emotional ostracism from others. Nevertheless, I urgently needed to ask deep questions, to have someone explain how they had "thought through" their beliefs.

I met my future husband in the early part of 1963. After a whirlwind courtship, we were married on June 25, 1963, at the home of a justice of the peace in a small Kansas town. Following a short honeymoon, we headed for the new life which lay ahead. As we traveled down the road toward our future, we talked about our aspirations and dreams for our lives together. Happiness seemed a secure ingredient in all our tomorrows. We were young, in love, and the future looked bright. I felt certain that together we could surmount any obstacles which might appear in our path.

I soon discovered that our apartment in the city was a very lonesome place. After living in the country most of my life, I found locating in the city a strange experience. A four lane street and stop light situated next to our apartment was a beehive of activity night and day as cars, buses, and trucks honked their horns, slammed on their brakes, and slid to stops thirty feet from our windows. In the distance trains could be heard clanking over railroad tracks as the sharp noise of their loud whistles pierced the air. Overhead the roar of jets could be perceived above the din of discordant sounds of the ground.

Sitting at our kitchen window, staring at the clamor below, I felt more alone than at any time in my life. When my husband was at work, there was no place to go without a car, and housekeeping chores in our small apartment were minimal. The solitude was frightening. I felt restless with too much time on my hands, too much time to think. Why did I feel so alone and so empty? I was beginning a new life with the man I adored; I was happier than I had ever been before, and yet, something was wrong. What was the missing dimension? At the time I didn't realize my soul could never find rest apart from God.

Dissatisfied with city life, we moved back to the rural area of our upbringing in 1966. By this time our family had increased to four, and we felt the country environment would be good for our children.

Our church attendance as a family was infrequent. My husband had also grown up apart from the church. Lewis was uninterested in going to church himself, but he had no objections to my attending. Although it was awkward for me to go without my husband, when our children were in primary school, the three of us did attend for a short time. Still feeling a need for God, I was hoping to clear up some problem questions concerning Christianity. But the minister never talked about matters I needed to hear. Instead, for the most part, he dwelt on subjects which concerned those who were already members of the church. He frequently talked about their need for spiritual growth and their moral obligations as Christians. Although I wasn't receiving the spiritual guidance I needed, I felt everyone was expecting me to make a decision. It seemed hypocritical for me to attend church if I was a non-Christian. We quit going.

Our children attended Vacation Bible School in the summers, and Lewis and I joined them the last night for closing programs like so many other families. These were the only times we went to church together.

Years continued to pass, but my spiritual dilemma remained unresolved. Many of my questions were still unanswered because certain subjects could not be discussed in-depth. The conflict between science and the Bible is a good example of this type of question which still bothered me and for which I had no answers. As a youngster studying science in school, I had learned of the great age of our universe. This knowledge presented a problem. Science textbooks inform us that the universe is billions of years old. I had been told it was the teaching of Genesis that God created the universe in six days around six thousand years ago. If the Bible really taught this, something was drastically wrong. Statements of the Bible would be in direct conflict with facts of science.

Where could I find the truth? I soon discovered that it was not permissible to ask about such issues in Sunday School or in church. Questions concerning the apparent conflict between science and the Bible were taboo. I was told that viewpoints contradicting logic had to be accepted by faith — even if they made no sense.

The years quickly passed, but the knots of my spiritual confusion remained unraveled. Although I had never previously expressed with our children my thoughts on the issue of a possible conflict between science and the Bible, I was surprised to discover that they had also wondered about the subject.

Early in 1982, Karen expressed her confusion on the issue. One morning, as the children and I were getting ready to leave the house, my daughter confronted me with the question, "Mom, do you believe in God?" David was listening and obviously interested in my answer. Shocked by her question, I replied, "Yes Karen, I do believe in God."

"Well," Karen responded, "My science teacher explained that science has shown the universe to be billions of years old, but the Bible seems to teach that it is only several thousand. Also, how can statements about evolution be reconciled with what the Bible says about Adam and Eve? How can I believe the Bible?"

"I don't know, Karen," I sadly replied. I certainly could sympathize with my daughter's uncertainty. Deciding to be completely honest, I continued, "I have never been able to find anyone who would answer those same questions for me. I wish I could tell you where answers could be found, but the truth is that I simply don't know." I went on to explain, "I do believe in God. It is just that these types of questions make me wonder if the Bible is his book; therefore, I don't know what religion to believe. I don't know what to think." I worriedly implored, "Karen, you do believe in God don't you?"

"Yes, Mom," Karen replied.

That was the last time we mentioned the subject. I pondered our conversation in my heart, however. My daughter had expressed doubts and asked questions which I didn't know how to answer. Where could I find clarifications? I simply didn't know where to turn for help.

In March of 1982, a few weeks after our conversation concerning science and the Bible, Karen was killed. A part of me died with my daughter. Now, I had to search for spiritual truth and answers — I couldn't bear to go on living unless I found solutions. I had so many unanswered philosophical questions. But where could I find help? Past experience had caused me to feel that I wouldn't receive the spiritual assistance I needed at church. Where could I turn?

Finally, the realization dawned on me that perhaps I could pray to God for help with this problem. If there really was a God, surely he would help me find answers. Three months after Karen's death, I got up from bed one night at 3:00 a.m. to ask for help in understanding. In desperation I prayed that God, if he was really "there," would help me in my search for spiritual truth.

Perhaps the case of the Ethiopian nobleman from Acts 8 will further explain my dilemma. While reading the Old Testament, the Ethiopian came to the book of Isaiah. Unable to understand what the Prophet Isaiah meant, the nobleman needed someone to interpret the Scripture to him. Aware that the Ethiopian was a sincere searcher, God sent his angel to instruct Philip to interpret the Scripture for him and to lead him to a saving knowledge of Jesus Christ. Likewise, God knew I was a sincere searcher. So many basic, unanswered questions remained in my mind, yet I was sincerely trying to search for truth.

A most remarkable thing happened the afternoon after my prayer for spiritual help. Previously I told about Karen and me reading together the *Reader's Digest* version of *Song for Sarah* by Paula D'Arcy. Soon after Karen's death, I bought the book version. I had noticed the preliminaries of *Song for Sarah* included a few words by a man named Sheldon Vanauken who was extolling the value of the book.

I mention this because of something which happened later the same day of my prayer for spiritual guidance. Deciding to go shopping at the large mall of a nearby city, I found my curiosity aroused when I "accidentally" noticed the book, *A Severe Mercy*, by Sheldon Vanauken, the man I just mentioned. Under the name of the book and the author were these words: "Includes eighteen previously unpublished letters by C. S. Lewis." Although I had never heard of C. S. Lewis, I assumed he must be someone very important. Later, spying a book by C. S. Lewis, I impulsively decided to purchase both books.

Back at home reading the two books that night, I was totally amazed. Sheldon Vanauken explained in his book how he and his wife went through a search for spiritual truth and answers. Corresponding by letter with C. S. Lewis, Mr. Vanauken asked many philosophical questions about Christianity, and Mr. Lewis answered the questions by letter.

It was remarkable that the Vanaukens asked C. S. Lewis some of the same questions which had been troubling me! For example, in *A Severe Mercy*, Sheldon Vanauken asked C. S. Lewis the question of whether Christianity is the only true religion. In an excerpt from a letter written to Lewis, Vanauken observes,

> *Very simply, it seems to me that some intelligent power made this universe and that all men must know it, axiomatically, and must feel awe at the power's infiniteness. It seems to me natural that men, knowing and feeling so, should attempt to elaborate on that simplicity — the prophets, the Prince Buddha, the Lord Jesus, Mohammed, the Brahmins — and so arose the world's religions. But how can just one of them be singled out as true? To an intelligent visitor from Mars, would not Christianity appear to be merely one of a host of religions?*[3]

As I read C. S. Lewis' answers to this and other questions, and as I later read his numerous books, Christianity started making sense to me.

C. S. Lewis was the *first* Christian I had ever encountered who shared how he had "thought through" or "reasoned" his beliefs. Reading his books, I could see real answers did exist to problem questions about Christianity.

The second book I purchased that day was *A Grief Observed* by C. S. Lewis, a personal narrative describing in vivid detail the author's experience of intense mental anguish suffered at the death of his wife. As I read his contemplative plaint on the sensations of heartfelt grief, I felt less alone. Here was someone who not only understood the dilemma of uncertainties and doubts, but who also knew the misery of deep sorrow.

Reading the epilogue at the close of his book, I was amazed to discover that C. S. Lewis had felt God calling him to become a Christian. Explaining the long route of C. S. Lewis' conversion experience, Chad Walsh writes that Lewis had perceived God's presence through events triggered by such things as "a bar of music, a landscape, a forgotten memory. The experience is an instantaneous sense of seeing into the heart of things, as though a universe beyond the universe opened itself wide for an instant and as instantly slammed its doors shut."[4] I immediately recognized the various descriptions of these experiences which C. S. Lewis had encountered and named "Joy."

After Karen's death, despite my heartache and confusion, at certain times I could deeply feel the presence and the love of God. My natural senses were sometimes heightened in an odd manner which transcended the limits of ordinary consciousness: sunsets seemed to surround me in an aura of light of almost unbearable beauty; lovely music had a sublime quality which was nearly heavenly. At such times, I felt the presence of God calling and drawing me to himself.

In numerous ways I had deeply sensed God's love and concern for me, but the most wonderful instance occurred in a profound way that will live in my heart forever. Searching for help one particular day, I was returning home in my car from a visit to a psychiatrist. My trip to see the doctor had been unproductive; I felt more despondent, more depressed in spirit than before my visit. Driving down the road, my thoughts on Karen, I heard a girl with a melodious voice singing a bittersweet song on the radio. Tears streamed down my face as she sang, "I'll see you again one sweet day." Suddenly a strange thing happened. For some unknown reason, I momentarily glanced up at spring rain clouds stirring in the sky, and in that moment, within my spirit, I felt God's presence comforting me and assuring me that the message of the song was personally true — that I *was* going to see Karen again "one sweet day."

Thinking back over everything that happened, I realized that events had been more than coincidental. I thought about the strange way *Song for Sarah* had led to a book by Sheldon Vanauken, and how that book, in turn, had directed me to books by C. S. Lewis, the great Christian apologist. It was not by mere chance that I had discovered those books. Without a doubt, I knew God had provided assistance in my search for spiritual truth. I had asked God for help, and he had answered my prayer. Finally receiving the spiritual guidance I so desperately needed, I was ready to experientially try Christianity. I accepted Christ as my Lord and my Savior in the summer of 1982.

A Reasonable Faith

1

What is Faith?

On an episode of *All in the Family*, Archie Bunker made this comment about religious faith: "It's believing something that you know ain't true." In agreement with Archie's sardonic comment, the television studio audience roared with laughter. In actuality many people do share Archie's opinion that Christian faith is an irrational belief in something that just "ain't" true. They assume faith is a blind and unintelligent act based upon superstition. For example, Robert Dean tells the story of the college student who felt his eyes had been opened to the fantasy of faith in God: "The pastor asked him what he thought faith was. The student said: 'It is believing the unbelievable, accepting something for which there is no proof. It is a blind leap in the dark, an act of sheer superstition.'"[1]

When believers fail to give reasons for the objective validity of their beliefs, they cause non-believers to assume that faith is based merely on gullibility. Even some Christian theologians are guilty of helping to spread this assumption. It is really not surprising, therefore, that non-Christians might attribute the Christian position to "sheer superstition"; especially when *some* twentieth century Christian scholars subscribe to a type of faith divorced from appeals to evidence or reason. Millar Burrows of Yale writes about existentialism, a brand of contemporary faith:

> There is a type of Christian faith . . . rather strongly represented today, [that] regards the affirmations of Christian faith as confessional statements which the individual accepts as a member of the believing community, and which are not dependent on reason or evidence. Those who hold this position will not admit that historical investigation can have anything to say about the uniqueness of Christ.[2]

Stephen Board concurs, "Much contemporary theological thinking

. . . is characterized by (1) a depreciation if not exclusion of evidential foundations for faith and (2) an emphasis on faith as an act of cognition, in which knowledge is furnished merely by believing." Board points out that expressions of this position run all through current literature on the subject. For instance, Eduard Schweizer depreciates the evidential foundations for faith when he observes that "historical facts never create faith, only faith creates faith." Voicing a similar conclusion on the subject of the historical Jesus, Jacob Jervell announces, "This conception of the person of Jesus [as divine Savior] rests on faith and not on historical knowledge." Confronted with the question of how one knows that God acts in history, Rudolf Bultman describes the act of God as something "not visible, not capable of objective, scientific proof. . . . The man whose desires to believe in God must know that he has nothing at his disposal on which to build this faith, that he is, so to speak, in a vacuum."[3]

Drawing its life from valid evidence of God's reality and power, Christian faith does *not* exist in a vacuum. Christian faith is built upon the solid foundation of what God has done in history. Clark Pinnock writes:

> *The Bible claims that God has revealed himself decisively in historical events. . . . Christians believe that the eternal Word of God became flesh in time-space history. . . . We believe this to be a fact capable of being tested and verified. We do not see it as an occult truth vouchsafed only to the initiated few, but an objective act of God in history which confronts all mankind with its force.*[4]

Really, it takes very little reflection to see that faith must be based on rational content. The only way we can know Christianity is true is if there is objective, historical evidence for the claims of Christianity. Only then can we have a personal experience and *know* that it is valid.

Nevertheless, many Christians insist that reason has no useful role in relation to Christianity. Many have interpreted Soren Kierkegaard, a nineteenth century Danish existentialist (1813-1855), as teaching that men and women come to experience Christianity only by a "leap of faith" with no reasonable basis.[5] Rather than giving reasons for their faith, people simply live it. It is even more saddening to realize that some evangelical scholars today think faith can be divorced from appeals to evidence or reason.

This attitude fails to take into consideration that our Christian witness involves not only "internal content" — how we live because of what we are within — but also "external content" — how we reply because of what we know. Christian life must be illuminating to the non-Christian both in word and deed, in knowledge and action.

Lacking external content, real knowledge of the objective evidence for the truth of Christianity, many Christians fall back on a type of faith commonly referred to as "simple faith." When challenged to give a basis for their faith, the only thing such people can do is retreat to a testimony of their "religious experiences" or their "emotional feelings." Mere statements of inward "experiences" or "emotions" are inadequate, however, to provide others with a clear base for Christian faith. It is very evident that "simple faith" is *not* really Christian, biblical faith.

Maurene Fell Pierson writes that simple faith, nonetheless, is particularly admired by many contemporary Christians: "Listen when church members gather for conference discussion and you are apt to hear more words in praise of simple faith than you hear in praise of God." Pierson explains that simple faith passes as an especially "fine" type of Christianity because "such an image supports the comforting conclusion that the acquisition of knowledge moves one in the opposite direction from faith."[6] Many even mistakenly tout this "simple faith" as real, true spirituality and knowledge as being unspiritual. Since there is little inclination for study in today's culture, this erroneous conclusion is valued and welcomed.

Numerous church leaders recognize there is an emphasis on simple faith throughout the contemporary religious scene. According to Paul Little, non-Christians and Christians alike are generally unaware of the essential relationship of faith and knowledge. Following his presentations of the gospel, Little frequently allowed discussion from the floor and was alternately gratified and dismayed by reactions from his audiences:

> *Unbelievers say the session has been helpful because it's the first time they've heard something that makes sense. I'm also gratified, but more deeply dismayed, when Christians tell me the same thing! They're relieved to discover that the Gospel can be successfully defended in the open marketplace of ideas and to discover that they haven't kissed their brains good-bye in becoming Christians!*

Little goes on to stress that in our sophisticated and educated world, "It is no longer enough to know *what* we believe. It is essential to know *why* we believe it."[7]

It is essential for Christians in our modern world to know why they believe, but Christian apologist C. S. Lewis (1898-1963) also states that he experienced *great difficulty* conveying to his audiences that Christian faith is based on rational content:

> The great difficulty is to get modern audiences to realize that you are preaching Christianity solely and simply because you happen to think it *true*; . . . This immediately helps them to realize that what is being discussed is a question about objective fact — not gas about ideals and points of view.[8]

In speaking to groups of people about "the value of knowing the scoop" in religious matters, Charles Swindoll often begins those sessions by saying:

> I am here today because there is a famine in the land — but not the kind of famine sweeping across India or sections of Africa. This famine is in America and most other places on earth. Not a famine of food or water . . . not a famine of churches or religious ministries. This is a famine like the ancient prophets mentioned — a famine of hearing the truth of the Word of God.[9]

This kind of famine does not involve a lack of churches or an absence of religious ministries; it entails a deficiency of "spiritual" knowledge. To support these statements, Swindoll often reads prophesies from Amos and Hosea that speak with incredible relevance to us today: "'Behold, the days are coming,' declares the Lord God, 'when I will send a famine on the land, not a famine for bread or a thirst for water, but rather for hearing the words of the Lord'" (Amos 8:11). "For the lord has a case against the inhabitants of the land, because there is no faithfulness or kindness or knowledge of God in the land. . . . My people are destroyed for lack of knowledge" (Hos. 4:1,6).

Unfortunately, many Christians fail to understand that it is the *neglect of knowledge which causes religious vitality to wither.* Elton Trueblood maintains part of the weakness of present day Christianity stems from the relative lack of emphasis upon rational belief. This deficiency has occurred both in the areas of literature and of ministry. Trueblood observes, "Christian books dealing with prayer and worship have been plentiful; books urging men and women to tasks of mercy have been abundant; but good books helping people to arrive at sound convictions have been scarce. " Books which seem to be concerned with belief often fail to provide clear answers; they only succeed in repeating the questions by which people are already troubled. Trueblood also states that "popular preachers stay very close to social issues and avoid involvement in the problems of ultimate faith."[10]

Shunning questions of ultimate faith, some ministers opt for *fideism*, the view that religious faith should not seek the support of knowledge. Trueblood notes that the major danger of fideism is it leaves the non-Christian with no basis for deciding the truth of differing religions:

> *This leads millions to the impotence of mere "fideism." The word means acceptance of "faith alone," with no concern for intellectual content. The crucial difficulty of this position . . . is that it provides no means of choosing between radically different faiths. It gives no basis for rejecting the Nazi faith or even the faith of voodooism. Once the life of reason is rejected, there is no reason why any one faith is better or worse than any other.*[11]

When churches fail to propound a rational basis for Christianity, they leave the door open for people to try cult religions. Jeff Amano, a research associate for Probe Ministries, says:

> *Many young people coming from conservative backgrounds become prime candidates for cult groups if the churches they attend do not teach effectively the how and why of their beliefs. Churches which don't teach reasons for their beliefs skim only the surface and stress a "milky" rather than a "meaty" comprehension of Scripture. This causes people to search for further answers.*[12]

Evidently many, many conservative churches are failing to feed the intellects of the young people they are supposed to be serving. Amano states that most members of cults are not "weirdoes who don't take baths and who have a penchant for airports and flowers. . . . Rather, cult members usually are above average in intelligence, between 18 and 25 years old, and are most likely to have a conservative religious background."[13] Unable to define their faith precisely because they have not been given a rational foundation for it, many intelligent youngsters from conservative churches are being drawn into religious cults.

Young people aren't the only ones searching for spiritual answers or being drawn into unconventional religions, however. Recent polls indicate a rising interest in spiritual matters among virtually all levels of American society, but this increased awareness does not seem to be reflected in commitment to Christianity. In *Who Do Americans Say That I Am?*, a study of American perceptions of Christ, George Gallup, Jr. and George O'Connell write:

> Some 3 out of 5 Americans today say that they are more interested in religious matters than they were just five years previously. . . . However, the new interest in religious and spiritual matters we see developing in the United States has not — at least until now — been reflected to any great extent in increased involvement on the national level. Church membership and church attendance continue to remain flat.[14]

After years of declining interest in religious matters, Americans are searching with renewed intensity for in-depth answers to the meaning of their lives, but polls suggest many are not finding needed spiritual guidance in America's religious institutions. Gallup and O'Connell stress that people today are desperate for answers and will look elsewhere for help if the organized churches do not provide religious direction: "There is a pronounced urgency in this because the renewed interest in religious matters could take (and in some instances, has taken) bizarre turns and lead [some people] to unconventional religions and cults."[15]

Another reaction to the lack of spiritual guidance in conventional churches is that many people simply become frustrated and give up their search for truth. In my own quest for answers, this happened to me as a teenager. And, most terribly it happens to so many teenagers in so many churches. Although a spiritual void existed in my life, I was unable to find anyone who would really answer my religious questions. Also, I was completely unaware of books that might have helped — I didn't know that books of this nature even existed. Thus, my search for God was postponed for many years. Only after a tragic event in my life, only after my young daughter Karen's death, was I able to find answers that satisfied both my heart and my mind. By that time I was truly desperate for spiritual assistance, yet I still didn't know where to find help. It was only by God's intervention in my life that I finally found truth.

There are two extremely important reasons why faith should be founded on reason. First, as stated, when faith is based on fideism, religious searchers are left with no basis for deciding between religions or truth claims. Second, "faith alone" is clearly unbiblical — the faith that the Bible requires is intelligent. Scripture commands us to "love the Lord your God with all your heart, and with all your soul, and with all your mind" (Matt. 22:37). God made us in his image with minds that can think through the nature of reality. He expects us to use that capacity to love and to glorify him. Loving God involves loving him with our minds, as well as with our hearts and our souls.[16]

During the course of Christ's earthly ministry, he challenged people to examine the claims of Christianity. On one occasion he turned to his disciples and addressed them with this question: "But who do you say that I am?" Jesus made his identity the crucial issue. His deepest desire, then and now, is for men and women to investigate his claim to be God, to know him as their Savior, to discover what life is all about. Jesus said, "I came that they might have life, and might have it abundantly" (John 10:10).

So, in the final analysis, what is faith? Is it believing something that you know "ain't" true? Is it believing the unbelievable, accepting something for which there is no proof? Is it a blind leap in the dark, an act of sheer superstition? It is none of these! A beautiful definition of faith is offered by Clark Pinnock:

> *Faith according to the Bible does not involve a rash decision made without reflection or a blind submission in the face of an authoritarian claim. It is the act of wholehearted trust in the goodness and promises of the God who confronts us with his reality and gives us ample reason to believe that he is there.*[17]

2

Is it Wrong to Doubt or to Question?

*S*ome Christians distrust virtually all use of reason or evidences to encourage faith. Why? Because they have been told it is wrong to doubt or to question — doubting or questioning is comparable to spiritual insubordination. Consequently, many people are afraid to admit they have religious uncertainties; not wanting to invite scorn from some Christians, these men and women just swallow their doubts. This is one reason why large numbers of people either give up on Christianity or look to unconventional religions for answers. Lloyd Ogilve writes:

> The aching problem, both inside and outside the church, is agnosticism. Many people "just don't know" what they think or believe in response to the awesome questions of life. Most of them are afraid to ask and even more frightened that they may be asked and be unable to answer. At the same time, they are troubled by easy answers and pat phrases that do not stand up to authentic spiritual and intellectual honesty. "Click words," esoteric jargon, and flip theories do not satisfy when life falls apart or tragedy strikes. There are far too few opportunities for Christians and honest inquirers to ask questions that have been lurking beneath the surface and to get straight-arrow answers.[1]

During certain periods in the course of history, men and women dared not communicate their uncertainties concerning religious matters; skepticism carried the death penalty. Alan Richardson writes that Christian philosophy was especially neglected "in an age in which the state orders all its subjects to be baptized in infancy and sends to the stake anyone who ventures to express religious doubts."[2]

Although skeptics are not sent to the stake today, there is very often a low-keyed rejection of those with questioning minds. In her article, "The Heresy of Simple Faith," Maurene Fell Pierson observes that one of "the damaging aspects of this heretical [simple] faith is its subtle persecution of those who do not want its product: these persons are variously labeled as atheistic, impious, irreverent, insensitive, and insincere."[3]

In my experience, the low-keyed rejection by some Christians of those who question is very subtle indeed. For example, as a youngster I once asked a Bible teacher a question about a possible conflict between science and the Bible. In a tone of voice which indicated to me that such questions would not be tolerated, the teacher answered my question by stating emphatically that one must simply believe such matters by "faith alone!" My teacher was letting me know he felt it was impious and lacking reverence for God for me to ask such questions. Of course, the teacher didn't have to actually call me an atheist or say I was insensitive or insincere. His tone of voice and manner were enough to squelch any questions I needed to ask. He didn't realize, however, that I was simply looking for rational grounds for accepting Christianity.

Many Christians assume the only thing that separates man from God is man's own corruption or sinfulness. The prevailing attitude is that human thought processes are so corrupted by sin that people cannot come to know God except through "faith alone." Philosophy is regarded as something men and women do in order to postpone or avoid faith; thus there is subtle persecution of those who express spiritual uncertainties or doubts.

In a similar vein, Edward John Carnell (1919-1967) writes that some churchmen insist that salvation entails a submission to the authority of the church, not to the dictates of reason:

> Some may rise to a final defense by asserting that it is our religious duty to submit to God's representative, whether we understand the reasons or not; for faith is a venture, a leap of the will in the face of paradox and objective uncertainty. To look for evidences is a sign of unbelief. Any delay will only increase our chances of losing eternal happiness.[4]

Carnell emphasizes that this idea is a "specious claim." God's children should never expect men and women to commit themselves without reasonable grounds. Christians are responsible to show others that "Christ's gospel is consistent with the claims of man's fourfold environment — physical, rational, esthetic, and moral and spiritual."[5]

The belief that "any delay will only increase our chances of losing eternal happiness" results in high pressure evangelism and in a questioning of the value or even the legitimacy of Christian philosophy. Christians are led to feel that it is their obligation to show doubters that they should quickly turn aside from reason and walk the path of faith. The historic Christian faith, however, is committed fundamentally to the concept of *objective truth*. For example, Paul observes (in dealing with the objective reality of the resurrection): "If Christ be not raised, your faith is vain;. . . We are of all men most miserable. But now is Christ risen from the dead" (I Cor. 15:17-20 KJV). It is also clear from elsewhere in the new testament that Paul never made what is called "a simple presentation of the gospel." Of course, he communicated as simply and as clearly as he could, but he states in Acts 20:27 KJV: "I have not shunned to declare unto you all the counsel of God." In other words Paul took the time to proclaim *all* the truth of the Christian faith. Likewise, we can do the same today.

Of course, doubt, in the face of *adequate information,* can be a smoke screen covering spiritual rebellion. But all intellectual problems are not necessarily the result of bad motives, however. Some questions result from the quest for a fuller understanding. Great numbers of men and women honestly search for answers and would gladly accept Christianity if only their doubts could be removed. For example, Jay Kesler writes about a college professor who expressed sincere questions about Christianity:

> *Non-Christians aren't always people in angry, sarcastic, argumentative rebellion against God. I find many like that professor, wanting to believe but not seeing that as possible. For them, it's important first to show that God is believable — that there is a good basis for accepting as genuine what Christ said. And perhaps they have special questions that need to be answered; this professor was a scientist and needed to be shown (probably by other scientists; through books) that there was no necessary contradiction between science and a belief in God.*[6]

This college professor had encountered data which did not seem to fit — he needed clarification that the findings of science and Christianity are not necessarily opposed. Christianity could only be true to him if it could be placed into some rational relationship to all that he knew and had to live with in the external world. Shouldn't this be true — isn't it true — of all of us. The professor was not attempting to avoid faith or to be disrespectful to God; he was simply looking for answers with which he could live. J. B. Phillips explains:

> Many men and women today are living, often with inner dissat-
> isfaction, without any faith in God at all. This is not because they are
> particularly wicked or selfish or, as the old-fashioned would say, "god-
> less," but because they have not found with their adult minds a God
> big enough to "account for" life, big enough to "fit in with" the new
> scientific age, big enough to command their highest admiration and
> respect, and consequently their willing cooperation.[7]

The human mind is endowed with an insatiable hunger for rational answers to questions about life — man's deepest needs cannot be satisfied unless his fundamental questions are answered. This is clearly true even for believers. Have you ever tried to explain the death of a loved one to someone who had no real understanding of the problem of evil and the Christian response? Consequently, doubt can be a prelude to spiritual truth; the seeker of truth can use his uncertainties as a motivation to find honest answers. As Peter Abelard (1079-1142) points out, "By doubting we are led to inquire, and by inquiry we perceive the truth."[8]

When non-Christians search for meaning and truth, the last thing they need is for Christians to pronounce judgment upon their doubts. Church should be a place, not where an unbeliever's doubts and questions are shunned, but where such problems receive sympathetic attention. When Christians dismiss the intellectual difficulties of non-Christians as if they do not exist, seekers of truth are left with plaguing doubts as to whether Christianity really makes sense.

The problem is complicated by the fact that some Christians have never practiced philosophical thinking — their faith has been acquired by a type of untested assent. Faith comes easily; it never occurs to them to doubt. These believers fail to realize that numerous men and women *need* for them to know Christian philosophy. Without a Christian answer, many people are left defenseless against the false philosophy of unconventional religious. C. S. Lewis observes, "Good philosophy must exist, if for no other reason, because bad philosophy needs to be answered."[9]

"Faith alone" is no longer meaningful in our world with its endless variety of religions; unbelievers need more than a mere testimony of a subjective experience as a standard for choosing between religions. In our modern world, men and women from many religious backgrounds testify to experiences in which they claim to have found ultimate truth. Josh McDowell writes, "The Mormons talk about the burning in their heart; those in Eastern religions will talk about the peace and tranquility they receive; others will admit to a new joy or happiness."[10]

Christian philosophy is needed to critique these non-Christian outlooks, to point out various problems with views that fail on philosophical grounds. Terry Miethe proclaims the many merits of Christian philosophy:

> *Christian philosophy can help the believer and the unbeliever to know the evidence for a Christian world view, to better understand the essence of the faith, to expose claims against the faith that are not true and to show — though all the evidence may not be in — that the Christian position is a credible intellectual position as against the counterclaims of its opponents. All of these are extremely important to the individual Christian and to the church. Christians, therefore, must be good philosophers.*[11]

Jesus has called Christians to be the salt of the earth. Among other things this means believers should offer alternatives to the ideas which exist around them. It is a grave failure of Christians to close off the possibilities for non-Christians to distinguish between truth and falsehood. If God's people won't stand up for the truth, others are left defenseless to resist the pressure of false religions. Christians should help mankind to see that great differences exist between Christianity and other forms of religion. The complete picture makes sense only with the Christian point of view. Other ways of looking at the world fall short — the pieces of the puzzle don't quite fit.

Is it really wrong to doubt or to question? Is it contrary to the teaching of Scripture to search for answers or seek for truth? The Word of God proclaims, "And you will seek Me and find Me, when you search for Me with all your heart" (Jer. 29:13). The word "heart" is often used in the Bible to refer to the mind or the human ability to reason. Turning to the Bible, we joyfully discover it is never wrong to think through or reason our beliefs, to search for God with our *whole* soul and our *entire* being. As Edward John Carnell points out, "Faith is a whole-souled response to critically tested evidences. To believe in defiance of such evidences would outrage the image of God in man."[12]

3

Is It Enough to "Just Believe"?

A familiar segment from Charles Lutwidge Dodgson's
(1832-1898) *Through the Looking Glass* presents a common view of
religious faith, the view that faith is contrary to reason:

> *"I can't believe that!" said Alice. "Can't you?" the Queen said in a
> pitying tone. "Try again: draw a long breath, and shut your eyes."
> Alice laughed. "There's no use trying," she said. "One can't believe
> impossible things." "I daresay you haven't had much practice," said
> the Queen. "Why, sometimes I've believed as many as six impossible
> things before breakfast."*[1]

When Dodgson, writing under the pseudonym Lewis Carroll, created
the piece, he was undoubtedly aware of its theological implications. The
passage promotes the act of belief rather than any real object of belief;
believing is the most important thing.

The ludicrous nature of this viewpoint is obvious — believing something will not make it true! Josh McDowell writes, "Belief will not create
fact. . . . I may believe with all my heart that I want it to snow tomorrow,
but this will not guarantee snow. Or I may believe that my rundown old
car is really a new Rolls Royce, but my belief won't change the fact."[2]

Truth is completely independent of belief. Without a rational basis
for faith, the believer would be in company with the White Queen in
Through the Looking Glass who could believe "as many as six impossible
things before breakfast." C. E. M. Joad observes there can be no believing that the intellect cannot justify:

Men have spoken of "the will to believe," a phrase popularized by William James. But divorced from reason, the dictates of the will have no authority and carry no conviction. One might just as well will to believe X as will to believe Y. The fact that one does believe X is, on this view, evidence of nothing but the fact that one wills to believe X. The willing of the belief has, then, no bearing upon the truth of that which the belief asserts.[3]

Unreflective acceptance of beliefs is impossible for many non-Christians — these men and women crave logical guarantees of the credibility of Christian faith. When searchers voice their questions or uncertainties concerning the objective and factual truth of the gospel, however, Christians frequently admonish them to "just believe" or to "just have faith." In the name of "faith," some believers discourage seekers from investigating the truth claims of Christianity.

Resorting to proof texts, "pat answers," and mechanical forms of witnessing, certain Christians emphasize schemes which tend to obscure real reasoning. When the results of such efforts are small, the blame is attributed to the hardness of the hearts of the hearers. Instead, could it be some of God's people have forgotten the Bible's command to always be "ready to make a defense to everyone who asks you to give an account for the hope that is in you" (1 Peter 3:15)?

The predominant viewpoint among modern Christians seems to be that reason and argument are useless as ways to bridge the gap between doubt and faith. M. Vernon Davis of Midwestern Baptist Seminary of Kansas City writes:

Someone has said that Christianity is much like great music. It really does not need a strong defense so much as it needs a good performance. A person is more likely to become convinced by seeing a demonstration of the "the real thing," than by hearing the most persuasive arguments for its truth.

Davis insists that the believer's daily walk provides the most "persuasive evidence of the truth of the gospel."[4] According to him, men and women should accept the message of Christianity merely on the basis of the testimony of the committed lives of Christians.

While it is certainly very important for Christians to show non-Christians "the real thing," that is, lives that are authentic and really alive; to somehow indicate that this "real thing" can or should be separate from knowledge and a reasonable faith is ultimately devastating to biblical Christianity. And, to relate "the real thing," to "a good performance" is misleading at best! After all, a "performance" — as in acting — is most often only a counterfeit of the truly real. Mormons reportedly live very committed moral lives as do many other non-Christians. The question remains: "How does one distinguish between 'daily walks' if not by reason and objective historical evidence?"

What has caused the prevailing contemporary view that Christianity cannot and should not be supported by rational means? Why do some folks deny that argument for the truth of the gospel can be helpful in leading others to belief in God?

Throughout the course of history, there has been a seesaw relationship concerning the faith and reason concepts. A balanced relationship between the two factors has seldom existed. During some periods, faith has been overly elevated; during others, reason has been excessively promoted. Gary Habermas, in Terry Miethe's *A Christian's Guide to Faith and Reason*, observes:

> *While philosophers should be students of the history of thought, we never seem to learn the error of countering one incorrect school of thought by advocating its exact reverse. In other words, we too often respond to one movement by encouraging the pendulum to swing too far in the opposite direction. Trends in philosophy verify this back-and-forth movement.*

Miethe and Habermas affirm the "equal importance of both the facts of the gospel and one's personal faith-commitment to them." Faith and reason are both important; yet Christians often devalue one or the other, "leading to extreme positions that endanger the very nature of the gospel. To unduly elevate faith has led to various forms of the 'leap of faith,' while the over-elevation of reason often leads to various rationalistic errors."[5]

Contributing to the latest swing of the faith and reason pendulum were "rationalistic errors" of the Middle Ages. Reacting against the excessive promotion of reason in that era, many modern theologians turned completely away from natural theology and focused on means such as religious experience and emotional feelings to foster a belief in God.

Numerous church leaders note that modern evangelicalism nursed on revivalism and gospel music has been little more than a mood-centered movement. Calvin Miller writes:

> *Christianity has too often had a merely emotional approach to worship. In the wake of neo-Pentecostalism, we have been prone to step up our emotions while gearing down our intellects. Revivalism can produce Christians infatuated with feeling their faith rather than knowing it. New converts often become satisfied with a gelatinous "chummyism" that shakes with fervor but is without substance. This naivete leaves us powerless to answer the skeptics. Ours are desperate times.*[6]

Oliver Barclay maintains "the current culture of the Western world is tending to put feelings so much before thinking that it has in some circles become hard to defend Christian thinking at all."[7] Many Christians today feel intellectual matters are irrelevant in the pursuit of Christ — emotionalism is more important than thinking about the basis for one's faith. It is not easy to convince such people that their faith should consist of more than good "feelings."

According to Francis Schaeffer, individuals can cause quite an uproar in modern Christendom just by mentioning that true faith is based on more than emotional considerations: "To say (as a Christian should) that only the faith which believes God on the basis of knowledge is true faith, is to say something which causes an explosion in the twentieth-century world."[8]

Deeply ingrained in the minds of many present day Christians is the idea that reason and knowledge are useless as evangelical tools. Terry Miethe notes that a lack of emphasis on knowledge is apparent in the Sunday schools and the preaching in many churches:

> *One might think from observing many Sunday schools — the lessons presented in them and the way we prepare for these lessons — that we in the church are unconcerned about Christians being educated in the faith, and that we are apparently against biblical/theological education altogether. . . . Look at the preaching in many, many churches. . . . We have heard so often, "We must preach the whole counsel of God" meaning we must preach all that He has commanded us (Matt. 28:20). But preaching the whole counsel of God is so very different than the kind that never does, in fact, give people the biblical*

meat necessary to mature in their understanding of Christian commitment.

Miethe goes on to stress that Christian "preachers *must* see the relationship between faith and reason and must be willing to spend long hours in biblical study."[9]

Man is a thinking as well as a feeling creature. Because his faith must be thought through as well as lived out, he must exercise critical judgment in the context of his beliefs. When ministers and lay Christians begin to recognize this important kinship of faith and knowledge, they will no longer find it necessary to ask non-Christians to "just believe." Obeying the Bible's command to be ready always "to make a defense to everyone who asks you to give an account for the hope that is in you" (1 Peter 3:15), Christians will not expect people to commit themselves without reasonable grounds. F. R. Beattie observes:

> *Christianity is either everything for mankind, or nothing. It is either the highest certainty or the greatest delusion. . . . But if Christianity be everything for mankind, it is important for every man to be able to give a good reason for the hope that is in him in regard to the eternal verities of the Christian faith. To accept these verities in an unthinking way, or to receive them simply on authority, is not enough for an intelligent and stable faith.*[10]

Today, there is desperate need for God's people to stabilize the faith and reason pendulum. For hundreds of years, Christians have been swinging to and fro, placing too much emphasis either on belief or on knowledge, seldom balancing these extremes. It is very important that Christians refrain from over reacting again. Habermas and Miethe warn:

> *Philosophical truth is frequently a delicate balance of extreme views. As mentioned earlier, we must be ever so careful not to elevate reason so that faith suffers, or vice-versa. . . . To suppress the biblical view of either faith or facts can have an important affect on the gospel. . . . The elevation of the leap of faith has progressed to the very point of denying the facts of the gospel, while the elevation of reason and the need for Cartesian certainty leads to skepticism. To balance both facts and faith is to be both more biblical and more practical.*[11]

True faith is a "whole-souled" response. Nels F. S. Ferre writes, "those needs of whole response must naturally include the needs of the mind for truth, of the heart for high emotion, and of the will for right and satisfying action."[12] For proper conversion to happen, the *total* personality must be yielded to God. Serious repercussions occur when any aspect of faith is ignored.

In the parable of the sower (Mark 4), Jesus tells the story of the farmer who sowed seed in different kinds of soil. The soils represent differing responses men and women make to God. In these verses Jesus first illustrates some responses that are *not* genuine "conversion" experiences.

Three improper responses are described — the intellectual, the emotional, and the volitional. Without the involvement of the emotions and the will, the purely *intellectual response* is comparable to the seed that "fell beside the road." Jesus tells about the person who has head knowledge but lacks spiritual insight or understanding.

Minus the assistance of the intellect and the will, the solely *emotional response* is likened to the seed that "fell on the rocky ground." Christ pictures the individual who has some shallow emotional experience with "God," but possesses no "root" or "depth."

Unassisted by the emotions and the intellect, the purely *volitional response* is akin to the seed that "fell among the thorns." Jesus describes the man or woman who makes a "decision" but fails to live up to it because the cares of the world choke his commitment as seeds are choked when planted among thorns. I have observed many cases where people make a profession of faith but later fall away. They jump on the band wagon of Christianity without really understanding what they are doing or why they are doing it. They may have what looks like a real conversion for a while — but in the end their "conversion experience" turns out to be spurious and superficial.

These responses — the intellectual, the emotional, and the volitional — do *not* represent true Christian conversion. Commenting on the parable of the sower, Paul Little notes that Christ indirectly warns us in the story against the use of evangelistic techniques which could produce those abortive results:

> At the outset, we must concede the possibility of manipulating human emotions in some circumstances. And we would have to admit that some evangelists consciously or unconsciously play on the emotions of their audiences with death-bed stories, histrionic performances, and other devices. Our Lord, in the parable of the sower, implicitly warns against merely stirring the emotions in evangelism.[13]

Likewise, Jesus cautions us in these verses against any diminishment of the intellectual content of Christianity. In this same vein, Richard Dugan observes, "Unfortunately, salvation has been reduced by some to a "plan" or "formula". . . . But praying even all the right words with the proper inflection will not touch God if it is not from the heart and the expression of the whole heart."[14]

Finally, in the parable of the sower, Jesus describes the whole-souled response of true faith — the proper reaction of mind to truth, of heart to emotion, and of will to action. Genuine Christian conversion is comparable to the seed that "fell into the good soil" bringing forth fruit thirty, sixty, or a hundredfold — a total and permanent reorientation of a life.

God has said we will find him when we search for him with *all* our heart (Jer. 29:13). Involved are our minds, our emotions, and our wills. Since proper conversion can be aborted by neglect of just one of these faculties, it is extremely important that all factors be stressed.

Should we stop using our minds and "just believe"? No! There can be no believing that the intellect cannot justify. As Edward John Carnell points out:

> *Whatever else faith may be, it is at least a "resting of the mind in the sufficiency of evidences." The extent of this sufficiency is measured by a cool and dispassionate use of reason. An upright man cannot violate the rational environment; he cannot believe logical contradictions. If a dispassionate use of reason assures him that he has no money in his pocket, all the existential heat in the world cannot induce him to act on the firm assurance that he is rich.*[15]

Faith is informed by and limited by knowledge. We can believe only what we intelligently apprehend. Accordingly, the most urgent task of contemporary Christians is to express a credible faith for modern mankind, a faith so stated that men and women can be convinced in their minds. Returning one last time to *Through the Looking Glass,* it will not suffice to take the White Queen's strange advice, "Try again: draw a long breath, and shut your eyes."

4

Is Christianity Just a Psychological Crutch?

"Religion is the opiate of the masses." This famous line from Karl Marx (1818-1883) captures the essence of a common view of Christian faith — religion is seen as an attractive intoxicant or drug for weak people who can't cope with their future on their own. Overpowered by the harsh realities of life, men and women use Christianity just like alcohol or drugs to survive in this difficult world.

According to the viewpoint, a religious person operates strictly from emotion to handle his needs and weaknesses; Christianity is a subjective experience that has no objective reality. People believe in God because they *want* to believe, not because they have a rational basis.

In connection with that idea, a parallel expression is often heard, "I don't *need* religion," as if the basis of Christianity resulted from the religious needs of mankind. The root of the statement is the assumption that man invents God out of the pressures of his human fears and weaknesses — Christianity is seen as just a psychological crutch for emotionally weak people.

To support the psychological crutch view, major critics of religion such as Nietzsche (1844-1900), Russel (1877-1970), Sartre (1905-1980), Marx (1818-1883), and Freud (1856-1939) have set forth various theories of the origin of religion. Although the theories differ in points of detail, they all contain the common thread or idea that religion owes its origin and its influence to the psychological needs of mankind. Kenneth Boa and Larry Moody, authors of *I'm Glad You Asked,* write that skeptics such as Marx and Freud have portrayed religion as something for the emotionally weak:

> *Marx saw the problem as economic; religion is the carrot on a stick used by the upper classes to keep the lower classes from revolting. The masses were kept in tow with the promise of a better existence in the next life if they persevered now. Freud and others related religion to the fear that comes from contending with natural forces. According to Freud, man invented God to help him deal with the dangers and unknowns of life. Now that man is more sophisticated and less superstitious, there is little need for God.*[1]

The fact is we all *do* have profound spiritual needs that only God can meet; belief in God is related to the basic human drive toward meaning in life. Human beings possess an inborn, almost irrepressible desire to discover life's ultimate meaning. In my own case, I had long felt a need for meaning and truth, a need for God. Yet this need was suppressed until the tragedy of my daughter's death made the need so great it could no longer be ignored. Without spiritual answers, my life seemed meaningless. I was desperate for truth; otherwise, I couldn't bear to go on living.

Seeking answers to basic questions about our existence is not particularly a sign of weakness, however. In their recent book, *How to Respond to a Skeptic*, Lewis Drummond and Paul Baxter observe:

> *Great thinkers like Rudolph Otto, C. A. Campbell, Anselm, and a host of others contend that the universal religious instinct is far from weakness or unrealistic, as the skeptic charges. Actually they realize that to seek meaning and God is to face reality "as we find it."*[2]

True faith is not the invention of cowards or the weak, but the unfailing resource of courageous men and women who have dared to face reality.

If we all have deep spiritual needs that only God can fill, why is it that some men and women do not seem to feel this drive toward meaning? The answer involves the fact that people find themselves at different places in relation to the basic human need for meaning and truth. Clark Pinnock points out:

> *Obviously there are many who do face up to the issue and conduct a search for meaning. . . . But then there are others on whom the question has not yet settled in full force. . . . If life has been good to them, they probably have some personal goals — in their job or*

marriage — which give them enough satisfaction that the question of deeper meaning seems a bit remote. Unfortunately, however, the realities of life have a way of ganging up on a person with shallow assumptions. Something almost always comes along to shatter the dream and raise the issue of meaning for them.[3]

As long as they are finding superficial pleasure in life, some people are not interested in searching for answers. Because a non-Christian can find temporary satisfaction in family, work, money, and other externals, the issue of the real meaning of life often seems quite distant. But that kind of contentment usually depends upon circumstances — when things go badly, such happiness fails. Pinnock elaborates:

Happiness based on worldly security alone is endlessly vulnerable to the "slings and arrows of outrageous fortune" which may come in the form of illness or inflation or the loss of a loved one. There are all manner of threats to the meaning of our lives both internal and external which can conspire to destroy it if it is inadequately grounded.[4]

The trouble with "happiness based on worldly security alone" is that it always proves to be a mere shadow; contentment grounded solely on temporal values is continually subject to the "slings and arrows" of life. Hardships and tragedies of our existence serve to remind us, however, of our need for deeper meaning and purpose, of our real need for God. Pinnock concludes, "The goodness and worthwhileness of life will always be threatened until it is located within the vision of an intelligible and purposive order of significance and meaning that cannot be shaken."[5]

When the "slings and arrows of outrageous fortune" strike, crippled people need a solid foundation that cannot be shaken, a *cure* rather than a crutch. Jesus said, "Therefore everyone who hears these words of Mine, and acts upon them, may be compared to a wise man, who built his house upon the rock" (Matt. 7:24). Instead of offering a religious crutch, Christianity proffers a true *remedy,* a relationship with Jesus Christ, the rock of life. Nevertheless, it has been noted that sufferers generally lean on a variety of false crutches rather than on Christ. Charles Swindoll writes:

I've worked with people for more than twenty-five years. And I've seen them in the worst kind of crises. . . . It has been my observation through the years that people usually do one of four things when they

*are faced with information like this. I think of these responses as
common crutches on which people lean. . . . Popular though these four
crutches may be, escapism, cynicism, humanism, and supernaturalism
do not provide any sense of ultimate relief and satisfaction. They leave
the victim in quicksand — more desperately confused than at the
beginning.*[6]

The first crutch is "escapism." Men and women often try to avoid
the harsh realities of life by running away either emotionally or literally.
Keeping busy through work, travel, play, or other activity, people refuse
to think about their situation, to let reality really sink in. Others escape
into an unreal world of drug or alcohol induced numbness to the
unpleasant aspects of life. And tragically, some lose the will to go on —
in a final bid to escape the pain, they take their own lives.

Second, there is the crutch of "cynicism." Preoccupied with the troubles of life, many people grow dark and cold within. Often they spend
the balance of their lives in disillusionment, resentment, and bitterness
against God. Dwelling on their suffering, men and women become
victims of their own lack of forgiveness — permanently angry at God,
they refuse to accept his help and his love.

Third, others turn to "humanism." By directing their thoughts toward humanitarian goals, these individuals defend themselves from serious reflection about life and death. They assume that if they live a moral
life, love others, and do good, their eternity — if there is one — will
turn out all right. In other words, they think they are "hedging their
bet." Hence, some people fail to come to terms with the real truth of
what could be learned from their troubles. And, sadly, their real need for
God remains unmet.

The fourth crutch is "supernaturalism." Trying desperately to cope
with their painful existence, others turn to the world of the occult — to
the realm of witchcraft, wizardry, satanism, or astrology. Or they turn to
mediums in their search for information from the other world. Evidently,
even First Ladies are not immune to this false crutch! Dealing in the
dangerous sphere of demonic powers, these individuals often reject God
(or any sources of true knowledge of God), the *only* provider of true
peace.

Peace is the longing of every human heart, but mankind can find
genuine fulfillment and peace only in God — Christ alone holds the

answers to our questions, our search. He is the final resting place of our worries, our tragedies, our griefs, and our cares. Jesus said, "Come to Me, all who are weary and heavy-laden, and I will give you rest" (Matt. 11:28). People seek peace and security in many different ways, but only in Jesus Christ can they find true rest. Paul Little observes:

> *The human spirit can never be satisfied "by bread alone" — by material things. We have been made for God and can never find rest until we rest in Him. . . . It is very moving to hear the testimony of those who have restlessly searched for years and have finally found peace in Christ. The current rise in narcotic addiction, alcoholism, and sex obsession are vain hopes of gaining the peace which is in Christ alone.*[7]

Without a belief in God, the non-Christian must logically accept death as his final end. He believes the realm of time and space to be the only reality; therefore, he considers the life of growth to death within that order to be the only existence. Consequently, human life is rendered meaningless — there is ultimately nothing to hope for or to believe in. But Christianity offers an unending and eternal purpose for life. Harry Blamires comments:

> *Christianity is therefore a very remarkable religion indeed. In the first place it says, "There is a state of being beyond time and space where God dwells eternally." But it does <u>not</u> go on to say, "So this life here in the natural order is not all that important. . . ." No, instead of that, Christianity goes on to say, "But this world of space and time has been visited by God himself. He became one of us. He demonstrated indeed that our passing physical life here can be involved with his eternal life beyond and above the universe."*[8]

Wonderfully, the supernatural reality "that our passing physical life here can be involved with his eternal life" has enabled me as a new Christian to rejoice even in the midst of storm, to transcend difficult circumstances. Recently my son David was involved in a terrible car accident where he suffered a broken back injury, and a few weeks later my husband Lewis was diagnosed as having diabetes. Although such situations can be difficult to cope with in an earthly sense, during these troubles I experienced an inner peace that defies natural understanding, "the peace of God" (Phil. 4:7). Of course, as a wife and a mother, I was very concerned about these events; yet God's grace was sufficient for me.

Thus, whatever the test or the trial, Christianity has given to my life a deep sense of purpose and meaning — for now and for eternity. As Nels F. S. Ferre points out, "Blessedness is living now in the peace beyond this world which we know shall transform all suffering into endless praise."[9]

But how does a Christian really know that he is not just a victim of wishful thinking? If the human mind is capable of infinite rationalization, how does a believer know that he is not self-hypnotized? Could it be true that Christianity is just a psychological crutch?

Concerning the question of the validity of Christian experience, the real issue concerns the objective truth of the gospel. Is there any valid, objective reality to our belief or experience? Is our faith *based* on genuine truth? In Christianity our personal, subjective experience is linked to the objective, historical fact of Christ's resurrection. Our belief is based on fact, not on wishful thinking. Because Christ rose from the dead and is living now, we can actually know him and experience him today. Barry Wood observes:

> How does the Christian know he is not self-hypnotized? Because in Christianity our changed life is caused by the real presence of the risen Lord Jesus. He is real. He exists. He was seen by others. There is historical documentation of his life, death, and bodily Resurrection. In Christian experience, there can be no lasting change unless He (God) is the true source of it all. We profess that God is truly there.[10]

The best argument for Christianity is the record of history; the facts about Christ's life, death, and resurrection are as well attested to as any events from antiquity![11] Those facts rest on the credible witness of men who were so convinced of the truth of their testimony that they were willing to die for it. In Christianity we have the actual entrance of God into the human scene in the person of Jesus Christ, and this entrance is verifiable by means of his bodily resurrection. This "object" of our faith is not just some fabrication of man's mind, but a physical, historical reality — Jesus Christ is really "there." Commenting on the historical nature of Christianity, Josh McDowell notes:

> The God of Christianity is not an imperceptible, unknown God, but one who has specific attributes and characteristics, which are revealed in the Scriptures. Unlike some of the religions devoted to a mystical god, Christians put their faith in a God who may be identi- fied and who made Himself known in history by sending His Son,

Jesus Christ. Christians can believe that their sins have been forgiven because forgiveness was accomplished and recorded in <u>history</u> by the shedding of Christ's blood on the cross. Christians can believe that Christ is now living within them because He was raised from the dead in <u>history</u>.[12]

5

Are All Religions True?

Christianity, according to some people, is just one of an assortment of religions which are equally right or correct. Although there are some technical distinctions within this variety of religions, all of them are, in essence, considered true. Thus, when Christians make an exclusive claim to the truth of Christianity, that position is often met with anger or shock at what some folks perceive as a narrow-minded or intolerant posture.

Why do so many men and women think it unlikely that Christianity could contain final truth? In our country under the principle of religious toleration, all religious systems are guaranteed freedom of expression and equal treatment under the law. With the principle of equal toleration has come the idea that no religion has exclusive claims to truth, the implication that equal toleration means equal validity. It is one thing, however, to protect the right of every religious person to follow the dictates of his conscience without fear of persecution and quite another to say that opposing convictions are all true. We must recognize the difference between equal toleration under the law and equal validity according to truth. Paul Little explains the difference between toleration and truth:

> We live in an age in which tolerance is a key word. Tolerance, however, must be clearly understood. (Truth, by its very nature, is intolerant of error.) If two plus two is four, the total cannot at the same time be 23. But one is not regarded as intolerant because he disagrees with this answer and maintains that the only correct answer is four. The same principle applies in religious matters. One must be tolerant of other points of view and respect their right to be held and

heard. He cannot, however, be forced in the name of tolerance to agree that all points of view, including those that are mutually contradictory, are equally valid. Such a position is nonsense.[1]

Religious tolerance today has reached the point where it is no longer a virtue but a vice, a cruel casualness to truth. It is as if we said to a blind man sitting on the edge of a precipice, "It doesn't matter which way you move. All routes lead to the same goal." Equally, no kindness is displayed if we tell someone that all religions lead to God.

Before becoming a Christian, I had often wondered if all religions were correct or if only one was true. Reading Christian apologist C. S. Lewis, I discovered that Christianity emphasized objective truth — real history, people, places, and events. If it is true, it is true for *everybody.* If it is untrue, it is not true for anybody. Jesus said, "I am the way, and the truth, and the life; no one comes to the Father, but through Me" (John 14:6). If Jesus said He is the only way to God, and some other religion claimed to be another way to God, then either Jesus is wrong or the other religion is wrong. They cannot both be right.

It is illogical to assert that all religions are relatively true, to say that they are all pointing in the same direction. How can all religions lead to God when they are so different? We can easily see this by considering the five great world religions: Buddhism, Hinduism, Islam, Judaism, and Christianity.

Religions of the East such as Buddhism and Hinduism have a markedly different conception of God than does Christianity. First, making no ultimate distinction between their god and the universe, Eastern religions teach that god is all and all is god: you are god; I am god; the grass is god; the dirt is god; the insects are god; everything is god. According to the Bible, however, God is not the same as his creation: "In the beginning God created the heavens and the earth" (Gen. 1:1). Second, viewing god as one with the universe, religions of the East see god as ultimately impersonal, as an "it," but Christianity teaches that God is personal: "For God so loved the world, that He gave His only begotten Son" (John 3:16). The God of Christianity has a capacity to love the world. Third, the impersonal god of Eastern thought cannot have any interest in mankind, but the Christian God is intimately concerned in the affairs of man. Jesus said, "Take My yoke upon you, and learn from me, for I am gentle and humble in heart; and you shall find rest for your souls" (Matt. 11:29).

As we have seen, the God of Christianity is not the same as the impersonal god or gods of the Eastern religions, but what about the Islamic concept of God? In Islam, we have a God much closer to the Christian concept, a god who is personal and transcendent, or separate from his creation. Are Muslims worshiping the same God as the One revealed in the Bible? In a philosophical sense there can only be one Supreme Being. But the characteristics of this Supreme Being are markedly different in Muslim teaching than in Christianity.

There are three significant reasons it is impossible that Islams and Christians are worshiping the same God. First of all, the sources of authority for the two religions are different. Muslims accept the Koran as their final source of authority and believe that the Bible contains errors. The Bible claims to be the inerrant Word of God, the final authority on all matters of faith. Second, the Koran portrays a different God from Christianity. The Islamic concept of God is called "Allah" and within his nature there is only one person. Christian Scripture explains that there is one God who has eternally existed in three persons — the Father, the Son, and the Holy Spirit — the doctrine of the Trinity. Islam rejects the Trinity and the New Testament teaching that Jesus is the eternal God, considering him only a prophet. The New Testament reveals, however, that Jesus is "the Son of God" (John 1:34). Finally, the Islamic religion teaches a different view of salvation. The Koran states that a person can be saved only by his own good deeds: "They whose balances shall be heavy shall be blest. But they whose balances shall be light, they shall lose their soul, abiding in hell forever" (Sura 13:102-104). Yet the Bible discloses that we cannot earn our salvation, for we need a Savior, Jesus Christ, who died to save us from our sins: "Not on the basis of deeds which we have done in righteousness, but according to His mercy" (Titus 3:5).

The Jewish concept of God is closest of all to the Christian. But, again, the sources of authority in Judaism and Christianity are not exactly the same. Even though Jews believe in the Old Testament, most Jews have never accepted that Testament's prophecies relating to the divinity of Jesus Christ or the New Testament's message concerning him. Jewish people are strong unitarians; they believe in only one God and only one

Person in the Godhead. Hence, Jews will not admit their God was the Father of Jesus Christ. Without a belief in the deity of Christ, however, proponents of the Jewish religion must stress salvation through works. But the New Testament strongly emphasizes that "by grace you have been saved through faith; and that not of yourselves, it is the gift of God, not as a result of works, that no one should boast" (Eph. 2:8-9).

The major difference between Christianity and other world religions is that Christ gives us forgiveness and cleansing as a free gift. In contrast, non-Christian religions essentially teach a "works" system of reaching God or becoming better. As Cliffe Knechtle observes:

> All the other major world religions teach that you must get yourself together. You must pray five times a day, give alms, fast, take a pilgrimage, use a Tibetan prayer wheel, not eat certain foods, observe the sabbath, go to church or live a decent life or one of innumerable other possibilities. . . . Christianity is different. God tells us we will never _earn_ heaven or _deserve_ a right relationship with him. We simply cannot live up to God's standards. Instead, God has taken the initiative. . . . Jesus Christ, the Son of God, died on the cross to take the punishment you and I have earned.[2]

In reaching down to mankind, Christ has done something for us that we could not do for ourselves. No other religion tells how God has taken the initiative to provide for our salvation; other religions are a matter of man struggling to find God. In Christianity God has offered us a free gift — forgiveness and eternal life.

But how should a Christian, on the basis of his unique knowledge of God, evaluate other religions? Are other faiths all wrong?

Christians do not say other religions are completely false. There are partial truths in every religious and philosophic tradition, truths that Christianity conserves. The God who revealed himself in Christ has not left himself without witness in the world. Every virtuous thought, every glimmer of light, every word of truth to be found in any religion is part of God's self-disclosure. There is an enormous amount of the moral and the worthy, the beautiful and the good, in other religions. But there are also deep-seated differences which cannot be disregarded or smoothed over. C. S. Lewis points out:

> If you are a Christian, you are free to think that all these religions, even the queerest ones, contain at least some hint of the truth. . . .

But, of course, being a Christian does mean thinking that where Christianity differs from other religions, Christianity is right and they are wrong. As in arithmetic — there is only one right answer to a sum, and all other answers are wrong; but some of the wrong answers are much nearer being right than others.[3]

Christians do not mean other faiths are wrong in the sense that they produce nothing worthy or beautiful. Christians mean that these other religions are wrong as the framework of ultimate objective belief. Also, insofar as these faiths do not provide the true substance of God's dealings with humanity, they cannot alone solve the human predicament. Other religions may embody some true awareness of God, but a follower of Jesus must regard him, and him alone, as God's decisive revelation of himself.

Christians stress the conviction that God has acted decisively in Christ. But Christianity is not stressing some supposed superiority of Christian believers to members of other religions. In the light of the cross, Christians have nothing of which to boast, seeing themselves as sinners, deserving of nothing but condemnation. But they see also that God has acted in grace to bring men to salvation.

In Christianity we are dealing with history. There is plenty of documentary evidence to support the claim that Jesus of Nazareth rose from the dead on the first Easter Day almost 2000 years ago and launched the Christian community.[4] His scattered followers did not claim merely that a corpse had been resuscitated; they believed that almighty God was incarnated as the man Jesus, that he suffered and died on the cross, and that death could not hold him! Christ's resurrection vindicates his claim to deity, his claim to be the way, the truth, and the life. As Josh McDowell notes, no other religion or religious leaders can bring someone to the knowledge of the one true God:

When it comes to eternal matters, we are going to ask the one who is alive the way out of the predicament. This is not Mohammed, not Confucius, but Jesus Christ. Jesus is unique. He came back from the dead. This demonstrates He is the one whom He claimed to be (Romans 1:4), the unique Son of God and the only way by which a person can have a personal relationship with the true and living God.[5]

At the core of the Christian faith is the assertion of the unique importance of the person and work of Jesus Christ. However, if Christ is the only way a person can have a personal relationship with God, are those in other religions who have never heard — or never heard with understanding — of the Savior inevitably lost? For example, if a Hindu were brought up in India in a Hindu Family and in his lifetime never heard any other view than Hinduism, what would happen to him?

The Bible proclaims that God is going to judge the world in fairness: "Because He has fixed a day in which He will judge the world in righteousness" (Acts 17:31). Although we do not know specifically how God is going to deal with people such as the Hindu, we do know that his judgment is going to be righteous and fair. C. S. Lewis writes that God's total activity is not limited to the knowledge of it we have from the Bible:

> God has not told us what His arrangements about the other people are. We do know that no man can be saved except through Christ; we do not know that only those who know Him can be saved through Him. But in the meantime, if you are worried about the people outside, the most unreasonable thing you can do is to remain outside yourself. Christians are Christ's body, the organism through which He works. Every addition to that body enables Him to do more.[6]

Missionary activity is imperative because Jesus Christ has commanded us to take the gospel to all nations (Matt. 28:19). Since Christ is Lord as well as Savior, a consistent Christian must carry out his command by either going out as a missionary or by preparing the way for others to go. It is the mandate of our Lord that those who have not heard do hear, that "the gospel be preached in every land and nation, to every tribe and tongue, to every living person. If this mandate were carried out by the church, the question of what happens to those who never heard would be a moot one."[7]

Are all religions true? Christians believe in the uniqueness of Christ because Scripture tells us, "There is no other name under heaven that has been given among men, by which we must be saved" (Acts 4:12). Paul Little stresses that Christians believe this because Jesus Christ taught it, not because they have made it *their* rule:

> A Christian cannot be faithful to his Lord and affirm anything else. He is faced with the problem of truth. If Jesus Christ is who He claims to be, then we have the authoritative word of God Himself on the subject. If He is God and there is no other Saviour, then obviously

*He is the only way to God. Christians could not change this fact by a
vote or by anything else.*[8]

6

Does the Bible Conflict With Science?

distinctly contemporary barrier to faith involves the relationship, or apparent conflict, between science and the Bible.[1] Numerous men and women who correctly see that a belief in Christianity is linked to commitment to the truthfulness of the Bible are disturbed by the account of creation in Genesis. The Bible seems to them to teach that the universe and earth were created very recently in six literal twenty-four hour days and that God created humans in a special act. But that interpretation of the Bible apparently conflicts with the widely accepted scientific view that the universe and earth are extremely old and that all of life evolved by natural processes from inanimate matter.[2] Thus many thoughtful minds are led to question the compatibility of knowledge obtained by scientific investigation of nature and knowledge derived from study of the Bible.

Of course, until modern times, there was little question about the length of the "days" of creation in the Bible story. It was popularly assumed that the cosmos was created in six literal twenty-four hour days only a few thousand years ago. Due to scientific study in the nineteenth century, however, it became increasingly clear that the universe was billions of years old. The question of a possible conflict between the Bible and science is therefore a comparatively recent problem, presenting a serious obstacle to faith for many individuals.

Although modern people, young and old, are confronted with this tremendous obstruction to belief, the church has overwhelmingly failed, up to this point, to deal in a satisfactory manner with the relationship between the Bible and science. Of the three religious approaches to the matter, two are incorrect but vocal, and one is correct but practically silent on this area of considerable concern.

The first approach, the "Liberal" or "Modernist" viewpoint, is completely unacceptable biblically. As Don Stewart notes, Liberals "teach that a person can accept the biblical teaching about God, heaven, hell, salvation, etc. without accepting the statements the Bible makes concerning historical or scientific matters"[3] According to this view, often referred to as "limited inerrancy," it is proper to make a distinction between theological and historical or scientific statements. But the Bible makes no such distinction, teaching that "All Scripture is inspired by God" (2 Tim. 3:16). The Bible also testifies that the Word of God is always true: "I, the Lord, speak righteousness declaring things that are upright" (Isa. 45:19). It is also very important to remember that the Bible does not claim to be a textbook of science.

Yet, by advocating an errant Scripture, Liberals are, in effect, denying the truthfulness of God's Word and seriously undermining the Bible's authority. Consequently, they have put a serious roadblock in the path of many unbelievers who are led by Liberalist doctrine to question the truthfulness of Scripture.

The historical view of the church is that the Bible, from beginning to end, is completely inerrant or infallible. Stewart points out that inerrancy means "that when all the facts are known the Bible, in the original autographs, will prove itself to be without error in all matters that it covers, including theology, history, science, and all other disciplines of knowledge."[4]

Stewart explains that the biblical doctrine of inerrancy is understood with the following qualifications: inerrancy only covers the original writings of the authors of the Bible; it extends to the writings of the different authors, not to the writers themselves; the doctrine of inerrancy allows for the Bible to be written in non-scientific descriptions; it also allows for different writers to describe the same events with different details; inerrancy allows for pictorial language and figures of speech; and the doctrine of inerrancy does not demand adherence to the strict rules of grammar. But the important consideration is that the Bible is the inspired Word of God and in its original autographs inerrant.[5]

Another approach with serious difficulties regarding the relationship between the Bible and science is held by a group calling themselves "creationists" or "creation scientists." Reacting against the Liberal approach, creationists have erred in the opposite direction — whereas the former reject the reliability of the Bible in the name of science, the latter seem to reject the validity of science in the name of the Bible. Roland Mushat Frye states that creationists, in trying to protect the inerrancy of Scripture, believe in what is called:

> . . . *a young-earth theory based upon a strictly literalistic reading of Genesis. These young-earth theories typically can allow no more than 144 hours to the whole process of creation, or, with the digital adjustment by which one day is taken to be a thousand years, they can extend that to 6,000 years. As for the total age of the universe, they allow only a few thousand years, up to a maximum of perhaps 10,000 or 20,000. Basically, that is the time scale with its many implications, which creationism seeks to impose upon our scientific and religious understanding. It differs radically from the long time scale — running into several billion years — for which scientists find abundant evidence in nature. It also differs radically from the understanding of biblical records held by mainstream religion and theology.*[6]

Frye stresses that creation-science dogma and strategy are rejected by religious denominations which represent the largest total proportions of Christians in this country. While these mainstream denominations affirm God's creation of the universe, they deny the eccentric interpretation of creation which creation-science seeks to impose. Davis Young agrees, "Christians have always believed, as they still do, that God created and sustains the entire universe. But many and perhaps most Christians regret, as I do, that the words 'creationists' and 'creationism' are being used today by a relatively small group for very special purposes."[7]

Although creationists are few in number, a minority, they have been extremely vocal in pushing their viewpoint. Edwin Olson observes, "In publications galore, this message [creationism] has been disseminated through religious bookstores all over America. It has been picked up by a diverse readership — pastors, speakers, youth workers, and Sunday school teachers."[8] Even though the creationist message represents a problematic understanding of the relationship between the Bible and science, it is heard by many people and creates the false impression that the viewpoint is the only possibility true to the Bible.

However, what is popularly believed by some vocal Christians is not necessarily what the Bible teaches. Davis Young notes that creationists have distorted the findings of nature in order to gain an accommodation with what they are persuaded is the only possible legitimate interpretation of the Bible:

> *They have tried to make nature say things it is not saying. Elsewhere I have documented that creationists have ignored data when convenient and have been very selective in the use of other data. They have attempted to develop a wholly new science. Their wholly new science agrees with their biblical interpretation, but it has almost nothing to do with the facts of the Earth, rocks, chemical element distribution, fossils, and so on, except in the most superficial way. Their theory of a young Earth and a global-flood catastrophe has been superimposed not only on the Bible, but on nature as well. Such an approach to the harmonization of the Bible with nature is no harmonization at all, for it harmonizes by ignoring the real world in which God has placed us.*[9]

Creationists have presented their theory before the public as in accord with Scripture and nature. People must recognize, however, that this modern young-earth creationism is problematic at best, and furthermore, that creationism, and flood geology have put a serious stumbling block in the way of unbelievers:

> *Although Christ has the power to save unbelievers in spite of our foolishness and poor presentations of the gospel, Christians should do all they can to avoid creating unnecessary stumbling blocks to the reception of the gospel. Some people who might otherwise be open to the gospel could be completely turned off by Flood geology. If acceptance of Christianity means accepting Flood geology, some will not want to become Christians.*[10]

The third approach to the question of the relationship between Scripture and science is held by "mainstream" Christian institutions. Liberals sometimes reject the Bible for science, creationists seemingly repudiate science for the Bible, but mainstream Christians accept information obtained both from the Bible and from scientific investigations in nature. These Christians contend that both the Bible and the scientific study of nature are sources of information about the origins of the earth and the universe, of life and of man.

However, though mainstream churches possess the correct doctrine, generally they have been remiss about formulating basic affirmations of that doctrine in ways which might commend themselves to a scientifically educated public. Langdom Gilkey elaborates:

> *One of theology's major tasks in the last two centuries has been to understand reflectively how religious faith . . . can be reinterpreted in the light of modern science. Yet, a satisfactory (i.e., intelligible) understanding of the relationship between religion and science has not permeated American church life (or, I might add, all of American society).*[11]

America's mainstream religious institutions have generally failed to organize scientific data and religious truth into a rational and understandable system, into a well-developed philosophy of science and religion available for consideration by the public. In America's bookstores there is a disheartening scarcity of accurate literature on the subject of the relationship between religion and science. I discovered that firsthand in my own investigation for answers on the subject. Visiting every religious bookstore and library I was familiar with in my area, I found an *abundance* of creationist literature but a *meager* amount of good literature explaining the relationship between science and the Bible. That was very discouraging. Consequently, it is my belief that although some people search diligently for knowledge on the subject, most are probably rebuffed by the scant information which is both available and readable. Hence, great numbers of unbelievers are tripped up by the failure of mainstream Christians to provide basic information needed for faith.

Non-Christians need to know that Christianity and science offer complementary answers to different questions. Science tells us what happens in nature and *how* it happens. Christianity reveals *who* is responsible for the natural universe and *why* it exists in the sense of the ultimate purpose of creation. Both are ways in which God reveals himself. Robert Dean writes that "Science legitimately examines the observable data of the universe and seeks to unlock the secrets of how the universe is put together and how it functions." In contrast, the first two chapters of Genesis were not meant to be a scientific handbook on the universe: "Rather, these chapters affirm God as Creator and point toward his purpose in creating. The rest of the Bible elaborates on that purpose."[12]

But does the theory of evolution contradict the belief that God is the Creator of the universe? Michael Green asserts that evolution does not rule out the possibility of a Creator: "Far from it. The theory of evolution sets out to explain how varied forms of life have developed from more simple forms over millions of years. Belief in a Creator sets out to explain the great Mind behind all matter. There is no contradiction between the two."[13] The theory of evolution, directed toward an explanation of *how* life began, does not necessarily presuppose the absence of a Creator.

Of course, all scientific theories are open to refutation, and it is quite possible that evolutionary theory might one day be abandoned. But Christians do not have to stake their faith on that possibility. Many of God's people believe that evolution is simply a process the Lord may have used to create living creatures. David Field and Peter Toon write that the Genesis account is not to be understood as "scientific:"

> *Those who accept the theory of evolution and also believe the Bible to be true, see the early chapters of Genesis as teaching fundamental truths about God and his relationship to the world in a form which would have been just as meaningful for people living in the time of Moses as it is for us today. These chapters contains principles which are always true about God and his relationship to our world. The form in which the truths are expressed has to be recognized as an ancient type of literature; it was not intended to be "scientific."*[14]

But doesn't the Bible teach that Adam and Eve were the first parents of all mankind, and doesn't that idea conflict with scientific theories about the origin of man? Although some scientists claim the human race descended from prehistoric ape-men who lived on earth millions of years ago, a more recent theory suggests that "we're all descended from one African 'Eve' who lived some 200,000 years ago."[15] A *National Geographic* article reports that molecular biologists working at the University of California, Berkeley, have discovered startling new evidence suggesting a common African origin for all mankind:

> *They collected tissue specimens from the placentas of 147 women of different racial backgrounds. They concentrated their analysis on the DNA, or genetic code, of a part of the human cell called the mitochondrion, which is inherited only from the mother. It had proved useful in tracing family trees. Comparing the genetic material, they found that it divided into two main groups, one of which consisted*

exclusively of African samples. That group contained the most variations, and the researchers concluded that it therefore represented the most ancient branch of the family tree. They deduced an African "Eve," the ancestor of every living person, who lived some 200,000 years ago. Her descendants they theorized, carried her DNA to the rest of the world.[16]

These biologist say that all living people have a common ancestor from Africa who lived within the past 200,000 years. If that theory is true, the human race is *not* descended from prehistoric ape-men. Thus scientific study does not preclude the possibility that God made the first man and woman by a special creative act and that from these two the whole human race descended.

Does the Bible conflict with science? Although each source of knowledge provides information that the other does not, where the two sources overlap they basically reinforce rather than contradict each other. First, only the Bible addresses the *who* and *why* questions. The Bible repeatedly indicates that "God created the heavens and the earth" (Gen. 1:1) and that He created human beings in His own image for the purpose of living in a personal relationship with Him and with each other. Second, both the Bible and the scientific study of nature provide some information concerning the *how* questions of origins and are not contradictory when considered on the basis of valid interpretations both of scientific data and of the Bible.

Of course, some ambiguities now exist between our understanding of scientific truth and our understanding of biblical truth, but as we gain more facts these conflicts will diminish. Jack Wood Sears observes, "If ultimate truth is ever attained in science and in our understanding of the Bible, I believe the conflicts will evaporate completely."[17]

The facts of nature and the biblical revelation must agree because both are ways in which God reveals himself. Therefore, as Davis Young points out, "The facts of the Bible and the facts of nature . . . do not disagree but form one comprehensive, unified expression of the character and will of our Creator and Redeemer. Nature and Scripture form a unity, for God is one."[18]

7

Was Jesus Really God?

Over the ages many people have suggested various answers to the question, "Was Jesus Really God?" To some Jesus was a great prophet, to others a fine teacher, and to still others simply a moral man whose exemplary life was worthy to be imitated. Another group states that he was the Son of God. Who is right? The question of the deity of Jesus presents a sincere obstacle for many men and women.

Among the religious leaders of history, Jesus Christ is unique in the fact that he alone claimed to be God in human flesh. Josh McDowell points out, "Buddha did not claim to be God; Moses never said that he was Yahweh; Mohammed did not identify himself as Allah; and nowhere will you find Zoroaster claiming to be Ahura Mazda. Yet Jesus . . . said that he who has seen Him (Jesus) has seen the Father (John 14:9)."[1] Jesus identified himself as far more than a great prophet or teacher; he claimed to be deity, to be God.

During his time here on earth, Jesus made some fantastic claims about himself — he claimed to be the eternal God, the Creator of the universe, and mankind's only Savior.[2] Of course, anyone can *claim* to be God. The real question is whether the Lord's claim is valid: was Jesus really God?

Before I became a Christian, I often wondered about the question of the deity of Jesus. Although I realized that there had never been a man like Jesus, I wondered if he was only a great man and nothing more. Reading the works of C. S. Lewis, I was able to see the fallacy of such reasoning. In claiming deity, Jesus closed the door to any suggestion that he was just a great leader, teacher, or prophet. As C. S. Lewis stresses, Jesus never intended that alternative to be open to us:

> *I am trying here to prevent anyone saying the really foolish thing that people often say about Him: "I'm ready to accept Jesus as a great moral teacher, but I don't accept His claim to be God." That is the one thing we must not say. A man who was merely a man and said the sort of things Jesus said would not be a great moral teacher. He would either be a lunatic — on a level with the man who says he is a poached egg — or else he would be the Devil of Hell. You must make your choice. Either this man was, and is, the Son of God: or else a madman or something worse. . . . But let us not come with any patronizing nonsense about His being a great human teacher. He has not left that open to us. He did not intend to.*[3]

In facing the claims of Christ, we discover there are only three alternatives (often referred to as "the trilemma"): Jesus was either a lunatic, a liar, or he was, and is, the Son of God. The truth of Christianity stands or falls with the validity of tremendous claims of its Founder. If Jesus was not divine in a sense in which no other religious leader has ever claimed divinity, if he was deceived, mad, or mistaken about himself, then nothing of the most universal of religions, Christianity, would remain.

What of Christ's claim to be God — is that sheer megalomania? Was Jesus a lunatic, a sincere, but self-deluded person who is to be compared with a man who calls himself a poached egg? If Jesus was a deranged man, how could he possibly be a great moral leader or teacher? If his claims are untrue, he is much less than great.

There are places these days for people who go about claiming to be personages such as Napoleon, Washington, or God. A self-deceived person of that sort would probably be institutionalized to prevent him from hurting someone. Yet, in Jesus, we find no evidence of imbalance associated with a deranged person. If his claims to deity were the result of insanity, symptoms would have shown up in other areas of his life as well. But the Lord displayed no evidence of imbalance in any area. In fact, he showed his greatest composure under pressure. At his unjust trial before Pilate, Jesus maintained the highest level of balance and composure. As C. S. Lewis maintains, "The discrepancy between the depth and sanity and (let me add) *shrewdness* of His moral teaching and the rampant megalomania which must lie behind His theological teaching unless He is indeed God, has never been satisfactorily got over."[4]

Another possibility is that Christ lied when he said he was God. Perhaps he claimed he was God simply to give weight to his teachings? Again, if Jesus was a liar, he disqualified himself from being a good teacher or a fine prophet. Josh McDowell writes, "Many will say that Jesus was a good moral teacher. Let's be realistic. How could he be a great moral teacher and knowingly mislead people at the most important point of his teaching — his own identity?"[5] Likewise, fine prophets don't make a practice of lying, especially about being God. There is a test to discover whether someone really is a prophet: is what he says true? If not, he certainly is no prophet.

It is inconceivable for Jesus to be a liar. This view of the Savior doesn't coincide with what we know of his life and teachings. Historian Philip Schaff (1819-1893) notes:

> *How, in the name of logic, common sense, and experience, could an impostor — that is a deceitful, selfish, depraved man — have invented, and consistently maintained from beginning to end, the purest and noblest character known in history with the most perfect air of truth and reality? How could he have conceived and successfully carried out a plan of unparalleled beneficence, moral magnitude, and sublimity, and sacrificed his own life for it, in the face of the strongest prejudices of his people and age.*[6]

Christ's moral attributes coincide with his claims. No mere man could adopt the stance of moral purity and maintain it over the course of a lifetime. Such a man would soon betray himself by exposing some imperfection or flaw.

If Christ were just a man, those closest to him should have found some human fault. Familiarity in all our normal human relationships will eventually reveal our weaknesses and blemishes. As pointed out by John R. W. Stott, that was not the case, however, with Jesus in his relationship with his disciples: "They lived in close contact with Jesus for about three years. They ate and slept together. . . . The disciples got on one another's nerves. They quarreled. But they never found in Jesus the sins they found in themselves. Familiarity normally breeds contempt, but not in this case."[7]

These close friends of the Lord, who had been with him throughout his public ministry, did not find one hidden fault in his character. Peter's verdict on Jesus was that He committed "no sin" (1 Peter 2:22). John's conclusion was similar: "In Him there is no sin" (1 John 3:5). The followers of Jesus emphatically agreed that he lived a sinless life. Furthermore, Christ was able to challenge even his enemies with the question: "Which one of you convicts Me of sin?" (John 8:46). No one dared to respond! Christ's moral purity was too magnificent and glorious for even his enemies to deny.

Christ could not have been either a lunatic or a liar because those viewpoints do not coincide with what we know of the depth and sanity of his life and teachings. The only other reasonable conclusion is that Jesus is exactly who he said he was — the Son of God.

What credentials did Christ provide to authenticate his claim to deity? Christ's power to heal sickness and to forgive sin emphasizes his identity. One day the Lord was preaching in a private home in Capernaum, packed solid with people eager to hear his message. Friends of a paralytic brought the man to see Christ but were unable to get in the door because of the throng of people inside. Consequently, they went up on the flat roof to let the paralytic man down with ropes to the feet of the Savior. In Mark 2:5-7 the story continues: "And Jesus seeing their faith said to the paralytic, 'My son, your sins are forgiven.' But there were some of the scribes sitting there and reasoning in their hearts, 'Why does this man speak that way? He is blaspheming; who can forgive sins but God alone?'"

The scribes were offended. As experts in the study of the law of Moses (*Torah*), they were knowledgeable of Jewish law and familiar with the passage in Isaiah 43 concerning forgiveness of sins. Maintaining that only God possessed authority to forgive a man his sins, the scribes reasoned in their hearts, "Why does this man speak that way? He is blaspheming."

Knowing their thoughts, Jesus quickly answered, "'But in order that you may know that the Son of Man has authority on earth to forgive sins' — He said to the paralytic — 'I say to you, rise, take up your pallet and go home'" (Mark 2:10-11).

Christ certified that he had the power to forgive the man's sins. How did he do this? He confirmed the invisible transaction (forgiving the man's sins) by a visible act (healing the man's physical infirmity). Christ responded with action the people could see. He healed the man's illness that people might know he had authority to deal with the man's sins. Lewis Sperry Chafer notes:

> *None on earth has authority or right to forgive sin. None could forgive sin save the One against whom all have sinned. When Christ forgave sin, as He certainly did, He was not exercising a human prerogative. Since none but God can forgive sin, it is conclusively demonstrated that Christ, since He forgave sins, is God.*[8]

Every miracle that Jesus the Savior worked during his earthly ministry was designed to prove to man that he is God. When John the Baptist sent two men to inquire about Christ's divinity, Jesus said to them, "Go and report to John what you hear and see: the blind receive sight and the lame walk, the lepers are cleansed and the deaf hear, and the dead are raised up, and the poor have the gospel preached to them" (Matt. 11:4-5).

Christ demonstrated a power over natural forces which could only belong to God: he turned water into wine (John 2:3-10); stilled a raging storm (Mark 4:37-41); and fed 5,000 people from five loaves and two fish (Matt. 14:15-21). He did these and other miracles as proofs of his divinity.

The words of Christ are another line of proof which establish his deity. Wherever Jesus traveled, crowds of people followed and listened intently to his message. Common folks recognized that there was something different about this teacher and marveled at the authority of Jesus' words. Christ's teaching manner was radically different from the method of the religious scribes and rabbis. The rabbis were revered persons in the land, admired for their meticulous observance of the law, but here was One who spoke with greater authority then they.

The procedure of those earthly teachers consisted in referring to the thoughts and teachings of others; they quoted first one great teacher and then another. In contrast, the teaching of Jesus was highly original. Instead of frequently quoting other teachers, the Lord offered his own insight into religious affairs: "And everyone who hears these *words of Mine*, and does not act upon them, will be like a foolish man" (Matt. 7:26). The people had never heard teaching like this before: "When Jesus had finished these words, the multitudes were amazed at His teaching; for He was teaching them as one having authority, and not as their scribes" (Matt. 7:28-29). These men and women recognized the difference — scribes taught them *from* authorities; Christ taught them *with* authority.

Christ's ultimate credential confirming his claim to deity was his resurrection from the dead. The resurrection of Jesus is the foundation stone for all that Christians believe and experience. The apostle Paul noted: "If Christ has not been raised, then our preaching is vain, your faith also is vain" (1 Cor. 15:14). Without the resurrection of Jesus, our faith would have no objective validity.

Did the resurrection of Jesus Christ actually happen? Does this unusual event have a historically acceptable basis? In considering such questions, some people wonder why the death of Jesus should have significance as opposed to history's countless other executions and martyrdoms. Others have died unjustly and inspired those who came after them. In a similar way, couldn't Christ's death simply have inspired his followers to carry on his cause?

The significance of the death of Christ as opposed to others is readily apparent. Jesus did not die in the service of a cause, as we normally use the word; he was not a leader whose death inspired his followers to further devotion toward the achievement of a common goal. On the "before" side of the resurrection, Christ's death had *none* of the effects we associate with an inspiring death. His disciples were not inspired into a revolutionary or retributive rage; they were utterly disillusioned by his death. During the days immediately following the Lord's death, they were a sorry, frightened group of men.

Suddenly they changed! In spite of their former doubts, these same disciples were out on the streets of Jerusalem fearlessly proclaiming the name of Jesus. What caused this sudden dramatic change? Only the bodily resurrection of Jesus could have caused the profound transformation of the disciples.

The disciples proclaimed the resurrection as sober historical fact.[9] Their claim was based not on speculation but on empirical truth. They observed the risen Christ, talked with him, and ate with him. The resurrection event was a public spectacle and a matter of public record — it was not done in a corner. That the Bible presents history on this matter is a fact beyond serious dispute. Lord Darling, former Chief Justice of England, examining the evidence from a judicial point of view, writes, "There exists such overwhelming evidence, positive and negative, factual and circumstantial, that no intelligent jury in the world could fail to bring in a verdict that the resurrection story is true."[10]

There is only one explanation that adequately fits the facts — Jesus Christ rose from death. If Jesus has risen, he is still alive and capable of entering the lives of those who invite him. Because Jesus is really "there," we can experience and know him today.

Was Jesus really God? Everything about Jesus points to the fact that he was not just a mere man, but God. The life Jesus lived, the works he performed, the words he spoke, his death and resurrection — all stress the fact that he is God!

8

Why Does God Allow Evil and Suffering?

*O*ne of the most pressing problems of our time is the poignant question of why innocent people suffer — why babies are born deformed or retarded, why there are wars where blameless adults and children are killed or maimed for life, why there are handicaps and diseases, natural disasters and tragic accidents, rapes and murders. Why does God allow such evil and suffering? Does he enjoy seeing human beings suffer? Or, is he somehow powerless to prevent it all happening? If God is all-loving and all-powerful, why did he make a world with so much misery and pain?[1]

At one time, living through the ordeal of the tragic loss of my daughter, I deeply questioned God's goodness. It was difficult for me to reconcile what happened to my child with the idea of a God who is love. Before I could accept Jesus as my Savior, I had to find some answers as to why God had allowed such enormous suffering to enter my life.

Likewise, the problem of evil and suffering, perhaps the most obstinate barrier to a belief in God, creates a genuine difficulty for many other men and women concerning Christianity. As Elton Trueblood notes, the problem keeps great numbers of modern people from faith: "So far as rational faith is concerned the problem of evil is our most serious contemporary difficulty."[2]

Throughout history folks have wrestled with the classical problem of why an all-good and all-powerful God would allow evil to exist. C. S.

Lewis voiced our apparent dilemma: "If God were good, He would wish to make His creatures perfectly happy, and if God were almighty, He would be able to do what He wished. But the creatures are not happy. Therefore God lacks either goodness, or power, or both."[3] In other words, either God does not care, or he is powerless to prevent the tragedies and sufferings in our world.

Is it possible to believe in a good, all-powerful God while living in a world shattered by suffering? Many sincere seekers would like to believe in a loving, omnipotent God but wonder whether such faith is reasonable. Do Christians have any valid reasons for believing in a God of power and of love? Christians have some solid grounds for believing that a God of goodness and power has reasons for allowing evil and suffering. Although the Bible, the source of our knowledge of God's character, does not present a complete and systematic explanation of the reasons for suffering, it does give some important clues.

First, the Bible teaches that God is all-powerful: "Behold, I am the Lord, the God of all flesh; is anything too difficult for Me?" (Jer. 32:27). God is certainly powerful enough to deal with evil. He has demonstrated over and over that he has the capability to end evil and injustice. Thus it is a grave mistake for us to question God's omnipotence. God *could* overpower the world. By wiping out men like Hitler and Mussolini and Hussein, God could stop wars. Our Creator could "zap" the vehicles of all careless drivers to prevent such people from driving. God could take excess wealth from the rich and redistribute it to the world's poverty-stricken masses.

But God has chosen not to intervene. Why? Is it because he is powerless to stop such events as wars, accidents, and poverty? No! Free will is the reason an all-powerful God does not hasten to remedy every situation. God's main purpose in creating men and women was to allow them to enjoy his love and to give them an opportunity to return it. But love is voluntary; it cannot be forced. Consequently, God provided mankind with what is usually called a free will. Of course, God could have made people like mechanical robots or puppets dancing on strings. But he wanted people who would really love him and obey him, of their own free choice. C. S. Lewis goes on to point out that if God exercised his power to stop every tragedy, men would no longer be souls with free agency:

We can, perhaps, conceive of a world in which God corrected the results of this abuse of free will by His creatures at every moment: so that a wooden beam became soft as grass when it was used as a weapon, and the air refused to obey me if I attempted to set up in it the sound waves that carry lies or insults. But such a world would be one in which wrong actions were impossible, and in which, therefore, freedom of will would be void. . . . That God can and does, on occasions, modify the behavior of matter and produce what we call miracles, is part of the Christian faith; but the very conception of a common, and therefore, stable, world, demands that these occasions should be extremely rare.[4]

In the process of giving us freedom of choice, God has chosen to limit his own power in certain ways. For instance, when God made man free, he thereby imposed a limit on what he would do in dealing with mankind. Freedom is a great blessing, but it is also fraught with great peril. While God allows men and women to make their own choices, he also allows them to reap the consequences of those choices. This is the clue to the moral evil in the world and the explanation for much of the pain and suffering that results from human sin.

A great deal of the suffering in the world is caused by human wrong-doing, by "moral evil." Thefts, murders, rapes, wars and so on are all traceable to our wrong decisions. However, many of our other problems are not of our own making. "Natural evil" is found in the effects on people of distortion in the natural environment — earthquakes, hurricanes, volcanoes, floods, many diseases, and other calamities — which bring untold suffering to human beings. How do we explain the natural disasters which so often wrack havoc on mankind?

There is also a sense in which God has given a certain freedom to the universe itself. Robert Dean writes that another way in which God has limited himself is by:

. . . placing us in a universe in which certain orderly processes are at work. This does not mean that ours is a universe that runs by ironclad, unchangeable rules. God is no celestial Clockmaker who has made the universe, wound it up, and now has left it to tick away according to its own mechanism. This is God's universe; he knows and cares; he sometimes moves in ways that seem miraculous by those who assume that natural laws are fixed and rigid. On the other hand, God

is not constantly intervening to change certain ordered processes of nature.[5]

God has set up certain natural laws and systems to govern the universe. For example, the law of gravity keeps us from floating off into space. But the same law will cause pain to someone who jumps from the top of a tall building. Of course, God *could* catch such a person. There have been times when God has done miraculous things to save lives; sometimes God makes exceptions to the laws of nature. But the majority of the time God lets nature take its course. Natural disasters are not intended to cause suffering:

> *Consider the hurricane, the earth's way of releasing pentup heat and energy. . . . The hurricane is not meant to cause suffering, but if people ignore the warnings of nature, they will be injured by hurricanes. The same is true of faultlines, such as the San Andreas Fault. Faultlines are necessary to keep the earth from just breaking apart. But if people insist upon building houses on the San Andreas fault — as they do — then they are going to suffer when an earthquake comes. Such suffering does not result from God's intentions, but comes rather from man's foolishness. We can either go along with natural forces and accommodate ourselves to them, or we can ignore them and be hurt by them.*[6]

God opted to create men and women with free will, to allow us to experience both the love and the joy, the pain and the suffering of our existence. Would we have it otherwise? God could have made mankind with a predetermined destiny, but then we would have been nothing more than mere robots. Only through the mechanism of free choice could humanity attain any significance or real worth.

Second, the Word of God teaches that our Maker is a God of love who cares deeply for mankind: "Indeed, the Lord will give what is good" (Ps. 85:12). Scripture emphasizes that God always has the best interest of humanity in mind in all his decisions.

In considering the question of divine goodness, is it God's highest purpose for humans that we live a completely pain-free existence? Would a good God want to prevent all suffering and pain? C. S. Lewis comments that when we think of God's goodness, what we really want is "a grandfather in heaven — a senile benevolence who as they say, 'liked to see young people enjoying themselves,' and whose plan for the universe was simply that it might be truly said at the end of each day, 'a good time was had by all'"[7] Such a concept of the goodness of God is based on the faulty assumption that a fun-filled, pain-free life equals happiness. However, genuine, deep-seated happiness is something much more profound than the fleeting enjoyment of the moment. Actually fun and happiness have little in common. Fun is the emotion we experience *during* an act. Happiness is the deeper, more abiding emotion we feel *after* an act.

Of course, there is nothing wrong with enjoying fun activities. Going to a movie or an amusement park, observing or participating in a sport, engaging in a hobby or a game, are fun activities that help us rest and relax. But these forms of fun do not contribute in any lasting way to our happiness, because their positive effects end when the fun ends. John Allan notes that the difficulties of life often bring us more lasting happiness:

> *Sometimes pain, stress, and struggle are actually necessary experiences if life is to be all it should be. It is often in trying times that we learn the most important lessons and get in touch with our feelings at the very deepest level. Looking back on my life so far, I can think of a lot of fun times; they were enjoyable, of course, and I wouldn't have missed them for anything, but they didn't honestly benefit me much. The deepest and most precious experiences of my life are all associated with times of difficulty and pressure.*[8]

True happiness is not precluded by suffering. There is a certain amount of pain involved whenever people are moving to a higher level of growth; often we learn some of life's most important lessons in the school of suffering. Lewis Drummond stresses that we should "see our suffering selves not just as victims but as students — students growing into maturity. . . . The object of life is not ease but the maturity of the human soul."[9]

Many people have had to suffer in order to turn to God. Until they lost their material wealth or their health or someone dear to them, they had no desire for spiritual matters. C. S. Lewis says, "God whispers to us in our pleasures, speaks in our conscience, but shouts in our pains; it is His megaphone to rouse a deaf world."[10]

In my own life, I realize that God "shouted" to me, "called" me, through my daughter's death. In Billy Graham's book, *Facing Death and the Life After,* there is a beautiful chapter entitled, "Why Do Some Die So Soon?" Referring to what C. S. Lewis said about God shouting in our pains, Graham notes:

> *No one likes to be shouted at, and yet God loves us so much that when troubles come, He is there to call us closer to Him. Children may be the little trumpet players who bring us to our senses, and to our knees. "Jesus said, 'Let the little Children come to me, and do not hinder them, for the kingdom of heaven belongs to such as these'" (Matthew 19:14 NIV).*[11]

Reading the passage, I understood that God used pain and tragedy to compel me to make a search for truth, however arduous that search would be. Hence, God brought good out of my suffering.

Although various kinds of suffering in life are inevitable, we must recognize that it is our reaction to suffering, rather than the suffering itself, that determines whether the experience is one of blessing or blight. We can allow suffering to drive us to Christ for salvation and the power to be Christlike in character, or we can allow suffering to drive us to bitterness and despair.

Is our "happiness" the chief purpose of God's creation? Is the best of all possible worlds one in which human pleasure and painlessness prevail? We must answer, "No!" For God to shield us from all suffering and pain would be to rob us of a greater good, to rob us of discovering the heart of God.

In thinking about pain and suffering, whether it be physical or mental, we must remember that we are not alone. God not only is aware of our sorrow and pain, but also suffers with us and for us. The Bible emphasizes the sufferings of the Lord Jesus Christ: "He was despised and forsaken of men, a man of sorrows, and acquainted with grief" (Isa. 53:3). The Word of God also stresses that Christ identifies with our suffering: "For since He Himself was tempted in that which He has suffered, He is able to come to the aid of those who are tempted" (Heb. 2:18). "For we do not have a high priest who cannot sympathize with our weaknesses, but one who has been tempted in all things as we are, yet without sin" (Heb. 4:15). The message of Christianity is that God not only loves us and hears our cries for help, he comes to us as a fellow sufferer. David Field and Peter Toon write:

> *God himself did not remain aloof from suffering, but in the person*

of Jesus of Nazareth entered the world and endured pain of mind and body on our behalf. Even though the world has gone wrong, God has taken responsibility for it. Jesus died for that very sin and evil which has caused the pain and distortion of creation. He died the death due to us, and when we suffer he enters into close identity with us, as someone who has gone through it all himself. Above all, his death was "for the sins of the whole world": he made it possible for there to be a new start, a whole new creation. His rising from death was the beginning of this — its fulfillment is still to come.[12]

Christians can respond to pain and suffering with faith and hope because of the redemptive power of the death and resurrection of Jesus Christ. We know that pain and death do not have the last word — beyond suffering and death are life and resurrection. Ultimately — when Jesus comes back again — all pain, suffering, sickness, and death will be destroyed forever. The Bible says, "And He shall wipe away every tear from their eyes; and there shall no longer be any death; there shall no longer be any mourning, or crying, or pain; the first things have passed away" (Rev. 21:4). Eventually God will transform this chaotic, unjust world into an orderly, just domain. The faithful followers of Jesus will enjoy everlasting life in that perfect kingdom.

In the meantime Jesus commands us to be agents of compassion and justice in a decaying world. We know that suffering can be redeemed and that we can be used of God to bring this redemption to bear. Hence, as Cliffe Knechtle notes, Christians should "use science, medicine, law, business, education, and any other tool to alleviate suffering, prolong life, promote justice, and enhance the quality of life."[13]

Why does God allow evil and suffering? Although Christians are able to see only a few threads in the grand tapestry of life and God's will, we are not left to guess about God's character. Looking to the cross, we know that God is love. Paul Little observes that life is like a fabric with:

. . . many edges which are blurred, many events and circumstances we do not understand. But they are to be interpreted by the clarity we see in the center — the cross of Christ. We are not left to guess about the goodness of God from isolated bits of data. He has clearly revealed His character and dramatically demonstrated it to us in the Cross. "He that spared not His own Son, but delivered Him up for us all,

how shall He not with Him also freely give us all things?" (Rom. 8:32).[14]

9

Is the Bible Truly God's Word?

The question of the authenticity of the Bible produces a serious hindrance to faith for many folks. These men and women wonder whether the Bible is a trustworthy source of information, a genuine revelation from God. Before my conversion, I often wondered about the question myself. Non-Christian religions also have sacred books which claim to be God's revelation. How could I know for sure that the Bible alone is truly God's Word?

A variety of objective evidence validates the Bible's authority as the true Word of God. Some data on which judgment about the Bible can be based includes its unity, its divine inspiration, its fulfilled prophecy, its historical accuracy, and its miracles.

One indication that the Bible is God's Word is its unity. Although the book was composed by men, its unity flows from its source in God. The Scriptures were written over a period of fifteen hundred years by about forty different authors displaying such widely varied backgrounds as the following: Moses was a well-educated leader; Joshua was a military general; Solomon was a king; Daniel was a prime minister; Amos was a herdsman; Nehemiah was a cupbearer; Peter was a fisherman; Luke was a doctor; Matthew was a tax collector; Paul was a rabbi. These authors wrote in different places: Moses in the wilderness; Paul inside prison walls; Jeremiah in a dungeon; Luke while traveling; John on the isle of Patmos. The Biblical writings were composed on three different continents — Asia, Africa, and Europe — and in three different languages — Hebrew, Aramaic, and Greek.

Considering the diverse factors involved, we would expect the Bible to be a confused and disjointed text, anything but harmonious. Yet the Bible displays unity. From beginning to end it relates one unfolding story of God's plan of salvation for mankind through the person of Jesus Christ — Jesus is the theme of the entire Bible. Josh McDowell and Don Stewart write:

> *The Old Testament is the preparation (Isaiah 40:3). The Gospels are the manifestation (John 1:29). The Book of Acts is the propagation (Acts 1:8). The Epistles give the explanation (Colossians 1:27). The Book of Revelation is the consummation (Revelation 1:7). The Bible is all about Jesus.*[1]

The unity of the Scriptures is a significant clue that the Bible's origin is divine. It is highly unlikely that the authors wrote the Bible on their own. The writers were highly diverse people, separated from each other by hundreds of years and hundreds of miles. Nevertheless, there is a unity which binds the whole together, a complete accord. The only reasonable way the sixty-six books of the Bible could have come together with such complete harmony and continuity is that the ultimate author was God himself.

Another reason we know the Bible is God's Word is because of evidence of its divine inspiration. The Bible is by far the number one bestseller of all history with untold millions of people considering it to be the greatest book ever published. No other book can equal its poetic beauty or profound wisdom. The Bible claims, however, to be more than just the world's greatest book — it claims to be written by divine inspiration, to be the true Word of God.

Yet there are those who contend that the Bible is only inspired in a way similar to that of all great literature. People holding the viewpoint of *natural inspiration* acknowledge the Bible has high ethics, morals, and insights but say the Bible is only an achievement on the same level as other great writings. The viewpoint denies there is a supernatural dimension to the writing of Scripture and claims the composers of the Bible were no more inspired than were authors such as Shakespeare, Milton, or Confucius.

The natural inspiration view is obviously inadequate. The Bible clearly claims to be more than merely inspiring literature. Two significant Bible verses speak to the heart of the matter. One verse notes that "All scripture is inspired by God" (2 Tim. 3:16). Another verse states, "For no prophecy was ever made by an act of human will, but men moved by the Holy Spirit spoke from God" (2 Peter 1:21). As Paul Little notes:

The Bible originated in the mind of God, not in the mind of man. It was given man by inspiration. It is important to understand this term because its biblical meaning is different from that which we often give it in everyday language. The Bible is not inspired as the writings of a great novelist are inspired, or as Bach's music was inspired. Inspiration, in the biblical sense, means that God so superintended the writers of Scripture that they wrote what He wanted them to write and were kept from error in so doing.[2]

Although the writers of Scripture were moved by God to record that which he desired, they were not robots through whom he merely dictated. Rather, God worked in a supernatural way, using each individual writer's mind, personality, and experiences to convey his divine message to mankind. Thus God, by his Spirit, guaranteed the reliability of the very words that were written without depriving the writers of their individuality.

The Bible is clear that its origin is divine, that it is not merely inspiring literature. Don Stewart observes, "The biblical doctrine of inspiration means that the Bible is God's accurate revelation of himself. Thus, the Bible cannot be categorized with other literature that causes the human heart to be challenged. It is inspired, not merely inspiring. It is the Word of God."[3]

A third way we can see the Bible is God's Word is the remarkable number of fulfilled prophecies it contains. In the Bible there are literally hundreds of prophecies foretelling persons, places, and events hundreds of years before their occurrence. Only God, who is outside our time-space existence and our finite knowledge, could foretell events in history with such absolute accuracy before they happen.

Prophecies of the Bible were not based on vague generalities. Modern fortunetellers give predictions such as: "Soon a handsome man will enter your life." In contrast, Bible prophecies were specific in detail, full of contingencies which couldn't be rigged in advance in an attempt to produce fulfillment. One of the best resources detailing the importance of biblical prophecy is J. Barton Payne's *Encyclopedia of Biblical Prophecy* (Harper and Row, 1973). This book contains 754 pages with 1,817 entries covering all the biblical predictions in both the Old and New Testaments, as well as a complete discussion of all 8,352 predictive verses in the Bible.

It is impossible for biblical prophecies to be of human or accidental origin. It is well known that forecasting a single event with only one detail affords a fifty percent probability of fulfillment by the law of chance. If an additional detail is added, the chances of successful prediction fall to twenty-five percent. Adding a third leaves only one chance in eight of a fulfilled prophecy. In the Bible there are over three hundred predicted details of Christ's first coming. Left to chance, there would be virtually no way predictions of this nature could have been fulfilled.

In addition, the prophecies of Scripture could not have been written after events and pawned off as prophecies, because in many instances the fulfillment of prophecy did not take place until hundreds of years after the prophet's death. In some cases the fulfillment came after the completion of the Old Testament and even its translation into Greek.

What are some of the incredibly specific prophecies of the Bible? Besides the scores of predictions concerning what would happen to certain cities, nations, and people, there are several hundred prophecies pointing to the coming of the Messiah that were perfectly fulfilled in Jesus Christ. David Dewitt lists some of those predictions:

> The place of his birth (Micah 5:2 and Matthew 2:1), that He was to be born of one called a virgin (Isaiah 7:14 and Matthew 1:23), His life-style as a suffering servant (Isaiah 53), His triumphal entry into Jerusalem on the colt of a donkey (Zechariah 9:9 and Matthew 21:4-11), the betrayal for thirty pieces of silver (Zechariah 11:12 and Matthew 26:15), His humble attitude at His trial (Isaiah 53:7 and Matthew 27:11-14), the piercing of His hands and His feet (Psalm 22:16 and Matthew 27:35), His being beaten and spit upon (Isaiah 50:6 and Matthew 26:67), the gall and vinegar they gave Him to drink while on the cross (Psalm 69:21 and Matthew 27:34), the casting of lots for His clothing at the crucifixion (Psalm 22:18 and Matthew 27:35), the burial (Isaiah 53:9 and John 20:28), and that He was to be called God (Isaiah 9:6 and John 4:25-26).[4]

The odds that one person could fulfill these Messianic prophecies by chance are astronomical, but Jesus of Nazareth fulfilled these and many more. The prophetic character of Scripture stands alone in its content, completeness, and accuracy; it underscores the fact that the Bible is the true Word of God.

An additional way we can know the Bible is God's Word is through its historical accuracy. The importance of the biblical story lies in its being real, historical fact. It is because certain events really happened that the Christian has grounds for belief. Therefore, the historical accuracy of the Bible is of vital importance to us. Is the Bible grounded and rooted in history? Historians generally apply three tests to any piece of literature of history to determine if it is accurate or reliable — the bibliographical test, the internal evidence test, and the external evidence test. In the interest of brevity, only the historicity of the New Testament will be examined here.[5]

First, using the bibliographical test, an examination of the textual transmission by which documents reach us, historians have determined that the text of the New Testament is reliable. It has more manuscript authority than any piece of literature from antiquity. John Warwick Montgomery observes, "To be skeptical of the resultant text of the New Testament books is to allow all of classical antiquity to slip into obscurity, for no documents of the ancient period are as well attested bibliographically as the New Testament."[6] Fenton Hort adds, "In the variety and fullness of the evidence on which it rests the text of the New Testament stands absolutely and unapproachably alone among ancient prose writings."[7] According to the bibliographical test, the New Testament is accurate, reliable history.

The bibliographical test ascertains only that the text we now have is what was originally recorded. The internal evidence test determines whether that written record is credible and to what extent. Again, historians have established that the New Testament account is credible history.

The New Testament writers were eyewitnesses to the historical Jesus and his mighty works. Peter says, "For we did not follow cleverly devised tales when we made known to you the power and coming of our Lord Jesus Christ, but we were eyewitnesses of His majesty" (2 Peter 1:16). The writers of the New Testament gave firsthand testimony. But, given the fact that the documents are an authentic apostolic witness, are they an honest account? Can we believe what the apostles said?

We can believe the apostles because not only did they claim personal knowledge of the facts, but they also appealed to the firsthand knowledge of critics and other contemporaries concerning evidence about Jesus. Don Stewart observes, "It must be remembered that not all of the eyewitnesses to the biblical miracles were believers. If the disciples tended to distort the facts, the unbelieving eyewitnesses would have immediately objected."[8] The best possible jury to test what the gospel writers said was their own contemporaries. If the writers had been contradicted by the facts, the people would have quickly repudiated their testimony. Yet their record went unchallenged.

The third test of historicity is that of external evidence. Historians seek to find other sources which substantiate the literature under question.[9] Once more, the New Testament stands as the world's most documented ancient literature. Barry Wood writes:

> There exists today a vast amount of material written from the first century through the fourth century which is either knowledgeable of or quotes from the New Testament. Such men as Clement of Rome (A.D. 95), Ignatius (A.D. 70-110), Polycarp (A.D. 70-156), and Irenaeus (A.D. 180) along with many others recognize the New Testament as divine Scripture written by the apostles.[10]

Combined evidence from the three tests — the bibliographical, the internal, and the external — leaves no doubt about the historical accuracy of the New Testament.

Miracles are another indication that the Bible is the Word of God. The Bible, from beginning to end, testifies that God has broken into human history and performed miraculous deeds.

But why should we believe in the biblical miracles? Aren't there many other religions that claim miracles as a basis of the truth of their faith? When the facts are considered, we discover that the miracles of the Bible are on a different level from those of other religions. Josh McDowell points out that miracles God performed were signs to testify of his existence and power or to meet a specific need:

> The miracle stories as recorded in the Bible are always for a definite purpose and never to show off. There is always a logical reason for them. For example, there were 5,000 people who were in immediate need of food, which was promptly provided by miraculous means (Luke 9:12-17). At a wedding feast in Cana, the wine had run out. The need for wine was met by Jesus, who turned water into wine (John 2:1-11). The miracles of Jesus were performed out of love and

compassion to those who were afflicted. They were also meant to be objective signs to the people that He was the promised Messiah, since one of the credentials of the Messiah would be signs and miracles.[11]

Miracles serve to confirm that the Bible is the Word of God. The basic purpose of miracles, to demonstrate God's involvement with mankind, extends not only to persons who directly observed the events but also to persons who subsequently read of them in God's inspired Word. Miraculous signs confirm the truth of the Word which is spoken about Christ, pointing men to him as the Son of God and the Savior of their souls: "But these [miracles of Jesus] have been written that you may believe that Jesus is the Christ, the Son of God; and that believing you may have life in His name" (John 20:31).

Is the Bible truly God's Word? Scriptures's unity, its divine inspiration, its fulfilled prophecy, its historical accuracy and its miracles all serve to prove that the Bible alone is the true Word of God. Billy Graham writes:

The Bible easily qualifies as the only Book in which is God's revelation. There are many bibles of different religions; there is the Muslim Koran, the Buddhist Canon of Sacred Scripture, the Zoroastrian Zend-Avesta, and the Brahman Vedas. All of these have been made accessible to us by reliable translations. Anyone can read them, comparing them with the Bible, and judge for themselves. It is soon discovered that all these non-Christian bibles have parts of truth in them, but they are all developments ultimately in the wrong direction. . . . Even the most casual observer soon discovers that the Bible is radically different. It is the only Book that offers man a redemption and points the way out of his dilemmas. It is our one sure guide in an unsure world.[12]

10

Does God Really Send People to Hell?

$\mathcal{M}$any Christians tend to avoid the subject of hell because they think questions about eternal punishment are simply smoke-screens set up by unbelievers to dodge the real issues. Generally, however, when non-Christians ask — "Does God really send people to hell?" — they aren't setting up a smokescreen, but simply asking a sincere question that needs a proper response. Their real question is, "What is God like?" Many folks honestly are not sure they want to give their lives to a God who they perceive as so cruel and uncaring that He sends people to hell.

Would a God of love really send people to hell? The Bible teaches both the goodness of God and the reality of hell and trying to reconcile these two truths presents a difficult problem for many people. On the one hand, Scripture emphasizes that "God is love" (1 John 4:8). From Genesis to Revelation, we find verses such as the following: "Just as a father has compassion on his children, so the Lord has compassion on those who fear him" (Ps. 103:13); "I have loved you with an everlasting love; therefore I have drawn you with lovingkindness" (Jer. 31:3); "For God so loved the world, that He gave His only begotten Son, that whoever believes in Him should not perish, but have eternal life" (John 3:16). Without a question, the Bible teaches the love, the grace, and the goodness of God.

On the other hand, the Word of God stresses the reality of hell. In fact, much of what the Bible says about hell is in Jesus' own words. Jesus used expressions such as "unquenchable fire" (Mark 9:43), "weeping and gnashing of teeth" (Matt. 13:42), and "their worm does not die" (Mark

9:44) to teach the horrible fate of the wicked. Other New Testament writers support Christ's ideas about punishment for the wicked after death. Positively, the doctrine of hell is a basic teaching of God's Word.

So, how do we reconcile the goodness of God with eternal punishment? The two truths, God's love and God's holiness, must be balanced. Harold Bryson states that overemphasizing either truth could lead to prominent distortions of God's character:

> *Stressing God's love to the neglect of his holiness presents the picture that God is a sentimental grandfather. . . . But the Bible presents God, not as a tolerating, gentle grandfather, but as a loving, kind father. Reading sentimentality into God's character misses what the Bible says about God's stern judgment. On the other extreme, some have presented God as a tyrant who enjoys seeing the wicked suffer; as a stern judge, anxiously waiting to give every person what he deserves. The Bible's picture of God has the correct balance. Jesus showed the Father to be one who knows, cares, and gives help to his creatures. . . . The depth of God's love for humanity is seen when he went to the cross. . . . Jesus presented God perfectly with a balance between God's love and God's holiness that explains his severity on sin.*[1]

The Bible declares God to be holy — God's holiness demands judgment and punishment for sin. But Scripture also reveals that God is merciful and loving; he has provided a way to escape condemnation by sending his Son to die in our place. Christ came to deal with sin on the cross, to offer forgiveness to those who want to be cleansed. Men and women who say "yes" to that offer are voluntarily allowing God to make them citizens of his eternal kingdom. But those who say "no" to God's loving offer have made their own decision. The eternal consequences of the rebellion of each unsaved person will have been that person's choice, not God's.

But what about those who have never heard the gospel, those who die in childhood or who are mentally retarded, and those who lived before Christ? Where do they stand in the eyes of God? It is quite legitimate for us to ask how God will judge these people.

First, will God condemn to hell billions of people who have never even heard the gospel message? Some people are sincerely troubled by that question. In an article in a recent Baptist journal, it was estimated that "of the world's population, 1.7 billion are Christian . . . Another

2.1 billion have been exposed to the gospel but are not Christian, and 1.3 billion have never even heard the gospel"[2] What is the spiritual fate of this estimated 1.3 billion who have never heard?

The answer is we do not know how God will judge those who have never heard. William Spurrier writes, "Some theologians . . . assume too much knowledge about whom God 'damns' or 'saves.' The fact is we do not know and can never know in this life."[3]

However, when thinking about those who never hear the gospel, we find comfort in Abraham's idea, "Shall not the Judge of all the earth deal justly" (Gen. 18:25) and in Job's observation, "Surely, God will not act wickedly, and the Almighty will not pervert justice" (Job 34:12). Although the Bible doesn't develop this theme as deeply as we would like, such principles enable us to trust that God will do the right thing. Clark Pinnock concludes:

> *There is a hard-line view on this subject which states categorically that there is no possibility of salvation outside an explicit faith relationship with the Jesus of the Christian proclamation, a view which would exclude the majority of the human race. Needless to say, this opinion has caused sensitive Christians much pain and posed an almost insuperable barrier to those who might otherwise be interested in the gospel. There is another view, equally ancient and capable of validation from the Scriptures, that holds that God deals with people where he finds them. If he finds them in paganism, as he found Abraham and Melchizedek, he can communicate with them in that milieu. . . . God has not revealed all his arrangements to us, and we are not required to speculate about the outcome of judgments God has not yet shared with us.*[4]

The issue is not with those who have never heard the gospel, but with those who have heard. God does hold accountable men and women who are aware of the Christian message. The Bible is clear about the judgment which awaits people who refuse God's loving offer: "He who believes in the Son has eternal life; but he who does not obey the Son shall not see life, but the wrath of God abides on him" (John 3:36).

Second, what is the eternal destiny of those who die in childhood or who are mentally retarded? I know from my own sad experience that a parent who loses a child desperately needs God. Yet that parent can be confused about the eternal destiny of their little one. They need assurance that their young child is safe in God's care. Otherwise, how could they turn to God themselves? Therefore, it is extremely vital that we confront the question of the fate of the young and the mentally retarded.

Although the Bible is not explicit on this issue, it does provide us with some principles which suggest that children and the mentally deficient are not lost. David Dewitt observes:

> Biblical evidence indicates that people unable consciously to choose Christ are not held accountable for rejecting Him. . . . Deuteronomy 1:39 reads, "Moreover, your little ones who you said would become a prey, and your sons, who this day have no knowledge of good or evil, shall enter there, and I will give it to them, and they shall possess it." The "it" of that verse is not eternal life; "it" is the promised land of Palestine, not heaven. But the principle is the same. Those who are not able to be accountable were not held accountable.[5]

Other passages also imply that Children and the mentally slow are in some special way kept by the power of God. In Matt. 18:10 Jesus warns, "See that you do not despise one of these little ones, for I say to you, that their angels in heaven continually behold the face of My Father who is in heaven." In Matt. 18:14 the Lord says, "Thus it is not the will of your Father who is in heaven that one of these little ones perish." Finally, in Matt. 19:14 our Savior emphasizes, "Let the children alone, and do not hinder them from coming to Me; for the kingdom of heaven belongs to such as these."

An inference based upon what we know of God as revealed in Scripture is that little ones and the mentally deficient are under the election of grace. The specter of a young child or a slow person suffering eternal punishment is entirely unacceptable in a moral universe. We could never conceive of a God whose nature is love, planning or allowing such a hideous miscarriage of justice. Therefore, we can believe that young children and the mentally retarded are accepted into God's presence on the basis of Christ's atoning work even though they are incapable of exercising personal faith in him. As Barry Wood points out:

> Children are innocent until they individually respond to God in rebellion. This statement would imply that children or the mentally retarded are not accountable. Only Gods knows when a person is ready for the gospel. Some retarded persons never come to the age of account-ability and are under God's watchcare, just like a little child. It is my

understanding that Children who die go immediately to be with the Lord, perhaps escorted by guardian angels (see Matthew 18:10) into the presence of God.[6]

Third, what is the spiritual fate of those who lived before Christ? How could any of them have come to a knowledge of the true God? The basis of salvation has always been the sacrificial death, burial, and resurrection of Jesus Christ. Although the saving work of Christ was future, God saw it from before the foundation of the earth. Not bound by time, the Lord applied the benefits of Christ's death to all who called upon God for salvation. As David Dewitt notes, God's plan to restore man to a relationship with himself has never changed:

The message of salvation in the Old Testament is the same as in the New. Man is described as a sinner separated from God (Isaiah 59:2) and in need of a redeemer (Job 19:25). The only way people could get to God was by grace (Psalm 6:2) through faith (Genesis 15:6), and not by their own works (Isaiah 64:6). The object of their faith was the personal Messiah (Isaiah 53:3) who would be God Himself (Isaiah 9:6) when He would come to earth as a baby (Isaiah 7:14). They needed to have faith in the Messiah who would come, just as we need to have faith in the Messiah who did come.[7]

The details of Christ's coming were progressively revealed. Each age has received more details, and even we who are living today do not see as clearly as we will when Jesus returns. But the essential message of the gospel has remained unchanged since God first revealed the need of a sacrifice to Adam.

Does God really send people to hell? From the Bible we learn that God trusts people with the power of choice: "I have set before you life and death, the blessing and the curse. So choose life" (Deut. 30:19). God gives every person the chance to choose either right or wrong, blessing or destruction. He forces no one to go in either direction.

God doesn't *send* people to hell. Men and women condemn themselves to eternal punishment because in their stubbornness they refuse God's way of salvation. Barry Wood elaborates:

God doesn't send us to hell. We choose our destiny, God doesn't. There is only one requirement for hell — unbelief. Only one sin damns us — unbelief. John 3:18, 19 says it well: "There is no eternal doom awaiting those who trust him to save them. But those who don't trust him have already been tried and condemned for not believing in the only Son of God. Their sentence is based on this fact: that the Light from heaven came into the world, but they loved the darkness more than the Light, for their deeds were evil" (TLB).[8]

God yearns to save men and women from the effects of sin. This is why he sent his Son, Jesus Christ, for our redemption. On the cross of Calvary, Christ took upon himself the sin of the world. He was made sin for us, and our guilt was imputed to him. There upon the cross, suffering the infinite penalty for our sins, our Savior said, "It is finished" (John 19:30). The wages of sin had been paid forever by Christ. Those who place their trust in him have his word that they will never perish. By dying on the cross, Christ has done everything appropriate and sufficient to make it unnecessary for anyone to find himself in hell.

11

Why Are There So Many Hypocrites in the Church?

Although the issue of hypocrisy is sometimes raised by non-Christians as an excuse for rejecting Christianity, there are other times when hypocrites are a genuine issue. Often an unbeliever has been truly disappointed and disillusioned by people who profess to be Christians but live ungodly lives, and this is a real barrier keeping him from becoming a Christian. At least the non-church member admits he is not a Christian; he isn't deceiving himself or anybody else.

Christians are supposed to be different, to be holy people. The church has set for itself high standards of love, of ethics, of service, of worship, of peace. Yet, almost daily, newspaper headlines reveal examples of ministers, deacons, or church leaders who have been caught in unethical behavior such as adulterous relationships, financial exploitation, or some other inconsistency with what they profess to believe. Also, in their own communities, non-Christians observe church members who seldom miss worship services, who claim to be concerned about the "spiritual" dimension of any problem, but who commit immoral actions such as extramarital affairs, financial dishonesty in business dealings, and other shameful conduct. It is no wonder unbelievers so often ask, "Why are there so many hypocrites in the church?"

What is a hypocrite? A hypocrite is an actor, a person who pretends to know God when he really does not. "The hypocrite is one engaged in intentional deception. He pretends to be more righteous than he actually is. The hypocrite is a moral playactor. He lives a lie. He claims to be free of faults which he practices covertly. His life is a guarded sham."[1] Religious hypocrites make a charade of faith, go through the religious motions once a week, but the spiritual reality in their lives is nil. They are not true Christians at all, just hypocrites playing religion.

But even as there are lost people on the church rolls who are not real Christians, it must be stated that genuine Christians can sin and fail God. Christians aren't perfect, nor do they claim to be. Those who have come to Christ in faith know they are not morally or spiritually superior. In fact, it is the awareness of their own shortcomings which motivates these folks in the first place to turn to Christ for forgiveness and help. As Billy Graham points out, all Christians fall short of Christ's perfection: "Jesus is the only perfect Man who ever lived. The rest of us are at best but repentant sinners, try as we may to follow His magnificent example; and the church is but turning a blind eye toward itself when it claims infallibility or perfection for itself or any of its members."[2]

The church cannot claim perfection for its body. Christians are as liable to make mistakes, to commit sin, and to do unworthy deeds as anyone else. The only difference is that Christians have admitted their failures to God and are actively allowing him to change their lives. Barry Wood writes:

> Being a Christian is not a claim to having "arrived." We are not supersaints sitting in judgment on the rest of the world. We ought to put signs over the doors of our churches which read, Welcome: Sinners Only, because that's the only kind of people there are. The only real difference between a saved sinner and a lost sinner is that the saved sinner has Christ helping him overcome temptation. But what a difference Jesus makes![3]

It is important not to confuse hypocrisy with sin. In fact, a biblical Christian is a person who admits he is a sinner. A hypocrite is someone who outwardly pretends to be good. The distinction between the two is important.

Jesus Christ had very stern words for people who were hypocrites, especially the religious leaders of the day: "Woe to you, scribes and Pharisees, hypocrites! For you are like whitewashed tombs which on the outside appear beautiful, but inside they are full of dead men's bones and all uncleanness. Even so you too outwardly appear righteous to men, but inwardly you are full of hypocrisy and lawlessness" (Matt. 23:27-28). The scribes and Pharisees made an outward display of godliness but inwardly did not know God. Seeking the plaudits of men, they took pride in their knowledge of the law and the rituals, but their self-righteousness kept them from seeing their own sin.

Today, also, there are religious pretenders in the church who think they are fooling others. But God cannot be deceived and will one day tell these modern-day Pharisees the awful words: "I never knew you; depart from Me, you who practice lawlessness" (Matt. 7:23). Christ uttered harsh words against religious dissemblers because of the enormous damage that hypocrisy can cause. When religious fraud is exposed in the lives of church members, many men and women are hurt, disappointed, and disillusioned. One hypocrite can cause not only the loss of his own credibility but also the credibility of others in the church.

Hypocrisy is a very serious matter. But just because the church contains hypocrites does not mean that all Christians are hypocritical. Kenneth Boa and Larry Moody note:

> *Hypocrisy, then, is a reality that has not been rooted out of the Christian church. But it would be wrong to condemn all Christians as hypocrites just as it would be wrong to condemn the medical profession because of wrong diagnoses and ineffective treatments, as well as certain instances of mal-practice. For every example of hypocrisy in the church, counter-examples of genuinely transformed lives can be multiplied.*[4]

Most church members are dedicated, genuine Christians. Non-Christians should not let the few hypocrites in the church keep them from knowing or worshiping God. No one ought to miss out on a relationship with Jesus Christ because of someone else's inconsistency and hypocrisy. Jesus offers his perfect righteousness to imperfect people who turn to him in repentence. How foolish it would be for anyone to let resentment against hypocritical behavior keep them from receiving this priceless gift.

In connection with the question of hypocrisy, people will sometimes ask, "Do I have to join a church to become a Christian?" Joining a church, being baptized in a church, or going through some ritual in a church does not guarantee anyone salvation. As John Allan and Gus Eyre point out:

> *Certainly it isn't churchgoing which makes you a Christian. You*

may attend a church all your life, sing in the choir, hand out the hymnbooks, teach in the Sunday school, and still not be a Christian. The New Testament constantly exhorts those who belong to churches to be absolutely sure that they really are Christians. "Examine yourselves to see whether you are in the faith; test yourselves." "See to it, brothers, that none of you has a sinful, unbelieving heart that turns away from the living God." It isn't how you spend your Sundays, but where your heart is, that decides whether or not you are a Christian.[5]

Actually, however, when a man or a woman becomes a Christian, he or she automatically becomes a part of the body of Christ, a member of the universal church. Paul Little observes, "Each genuine Christian, regardless of denomination, is spiritually one with every other believer. All are in the Church Universal. We are united in Christ, who is our life."[6]

The New Testament Church is defined in two ways. First, it is the whole company of regenerate persons in heaven and on earth. The universal, invisible church includes all true believers in every place, those who have gone on as well as those still living. Second, it is the individual local church through which the universal church is evident. While there is actually only one universal church, there can be any number of local churches formed into various denominations.

So, what really unites believers is not an identical outlook on doctrinal matters but the experience of new life which forms a genuine, invisible bond between real Christians. Billy Graham writes:

Jesus Christ is the head of this great universal church. . . . It is upon His orders that the church has its existence. . . . The church has been widely criticized for many internal squabbles, much hair-splitting and apparent lack of unity. These, however, are superficial things: these are the conflicts that come from the slightly varying interpretations of the general's orders. . . . Study the underlying beliefs of the various denominations and you will find that basically and historically they are almost identical. They may differ widely in ritual, they may seem to lock horns over theological technicalities; but fundamentally they all recognize Jesus Christ as God incarnate, who died upon the cross and rose again that man might have salvation — and that is the all-important fact to all humanity.[7]

What is the church? It is the whole company of regenerate persons, not a particular denomination. Of course, the basic doctrine, teaching, and practice of a church must be in accordance with the Word of God. As Pat Robertson stresses:

> *The new Christian needs to find a fellowship of believers who love the Lord and who believe the Bible. There are Episcopal priests who love God with all their hearts, who are filled with the Holy Spirit, who serve Jesus, and whose churches are beautiful places of worship. In some Catholic churches born again Christians could feel at home. There are Baptist churches where the members love God, Presbyterian churches where the members love God, as well as Methodist, Assemblies of God, Nazarene, and Holiness churches and many others where the members love God.*[8]

Robertson goes on to state that new Christians should beware, however, of cult groups such as the Mormons, the Jehovah's Witnesses, the Unitarians, the Unification church, the Hare Krishnas, and the other fringe groups whose doctrines are not in accord with God's Word.

Does a person have to join a church to become a Christian? Joining a local church does not make a man or woman a Christian. However, as members of the universal church, believers are called upon to obey Christ, to follow his command to join with others in the worship of God: "Not forsaking our own assembling together, as is the habit of some" (Heb. 10:25). If we are obedient to our Savior, we will identify with a Bible believing local church and join other believers there for worship and service.

Along with the need for obedience to our Lord's command, there are several other reasons why Christians should attend church. First, the local congregation is the ideal environment for growth in spiritual maturity. There the Christian receives the proper admixture of worship, fellowship, and instruction. Those who continue faithfully in attendance will hear encouragement and exhortation and reproof that will keep their lives in line.

Second, the community church is the only place where believers can observe the sacred ordinances. Charles Swindoll writes about these beautiful sacraments or celebrations, so sacred to all Christians:

> *One is called the Lord's Supper (your church may call it Communion, the Eucharist, or simply the Table). The other is baptism. The Lord's Supper is a memorial of remembrance, and baptism is a cele-*

bration of reflection. With no desire to offend anyone, I sometimes think of them as sacred pantomimes. They are sermons without words . . . full of symbolic significance. The Lord's Supper is saying, "He died for me." The baptismal celebration is saying, "He lives in me." [9]

Third, the local church is conducive to the spreading of the gospel and for social service. In the words of John Allan and Gus Eyre, church "is a place where people can commit themselves together to hard work — to learning to live in love with one another, to sharing Christ's love with a hungry world, to offering new life to broken men and women, to working for justice and freedom and equality for all humanity." [10]

Fourth, the church is a place where believers can gather with others to help effect changes and improvements. Barry Wood encourages people to "come follow Christ and help improve the Church by being a better Christian than any you've seen. Rather than stand in judgment of the hypocrite, why not give yourself to Jesus and show the world what it really means to follow the Savior." [11]

Why are there so many hypocrites in the church? We must remember that there is a real sense in which all of us are hypocrites to a certain degree. Jesus said, "And you shall love the Lord your God with all your heart, and with all your soul, and with all your mind, and with all your strength. The second [commandment] is this, You shall love your neighbor as yourself" (Mark 12:30-31). We all agree that Christ's words are the standard for life. Yet none of us lives up to those words. Philip Yancey and Tim Stafford conclude that the greatest difference between a real Christian and a hypocrite is in our attitude toward failure:

Jesus once told a story about two men who prayed. The first man, a hypocritical religious leader, thanked God for the moral character he lived, which was considerably above the norm. The other man, a notorious crook, was so ashamed of himself he could barely speak to God. He did not thank God for anything. All he asked for was mercy. Jesus commented that the second man, not the first, was pleasing to God. The man was not pleasing because he had sinned less, but because of his humble attitude. [12]

12

Is There Need for a "Christian Reformation?"

Some churchmen insist there is need for a "New Reformation" of the church, for a change in approach towards Christian evangelism. Why? Because contemporary man is presented with an assortment of modern problems which loom as serious barriers to faith — non-Christians in our culture are surrounded by various forms of thought which make it almost impossible for them to seriously consider Christianity.

Various modern barriers — the concept of faith as an emotional experience; the notion that belief is just a psychological crutch; the trend of today's culture towards religious relativism; the apparent conflict between science and the Bible; and the various philosophical objections such as the question of the deity of Jesus and the problem of evil and suffering — pose genuine intellectual obstructions to faith for millions of honest searchers. Francis Schaeffer suggests that in our generation almost all people are affected by these problems:

> *If people do not have "modern" intellectual questions, there is no need of dealing with such questions; but we must acknowledge that in our generation almost everybody has them. I walked out of the restaurant one morning a few weeks ago, and there was a girl sitting with a cup of coffee reading Skinner's book Beyond Freedom and Dignity. She represents millions. We have millions and millions facing these questions, and in fact I think today the majority of the commu-*

nity have such questions. And they do not have to be university graduates. I have worked with shipyard workers, mill workers, all kinds of people . . . and I am convinced that these people often have the same questions as the intellectual.[1]

Millions of people in our generation face genuine philosophical difficulties regarding the truthfulness of Christianity. In this regard it must be emphasized that there are two separate meanings to the word *philosophy*. One meaning defines the term as an academic subject, a highly technical course of study in which few people engage. Schaeffer elaborates that there is a second meaning that affects the problem of spreading the gospel in our modern world: "For philosophy also means a person's *world-view*. In this sense, all people are philosophers, for all people have a world-view. This is as true of the man digging a ditch as it is of the philosopher in the university."[2]

Although the majority of men and women in our day confront philosophic questions regarding religious issues, Evangelical Christians have tended to despise the concept of philosophy, thinking of it mainly in terms of the first meaning. Therefore, one of the major weaknesses of today's evangelical, orthodox Christianity is the downplaying of the importance of philosophical issues.[3]

Of course, numerous people become Christians just by believing on authority, but that should not minimize the fact that millions of non-Christians *do* need to ask and to receive answers to in-depth questions concerning the nature of ultimate reality. Schaeffer comments:

> *At all points in the conversation, we must allow him [the non-Christian] to ask any question he wants. We cannot say, on the one hand, that we believe in the unity of truth and then, on the other hand, suddenly withdraw from the discussion and tell him to believe on blind authority. He has a right to ask questions. It is perfectly true that not all Christians proceed in this way with all modern people, and yet people are brought to Christ by them. For every person who is saved we should be very thankful. But to withdraw by saying or implying, "Keep quiet and just believe" may later lead to spiritual weakness, even if the person does become a Christian, for it will leave crucial questions unanswered.*[4]

Christians bear a responsibility to communicate their faith in such a way that religious searchers can achieve a whole-souled response to the gospel. In this process of faith-sharing, Christians will undoubtedly encounter non-Christians in various stages of need and they must respond to such people on that basis. For example, if a searcher is ready for conversion on the foundation of previous knowledge, that person may not have any questions. In this case it would be proper to immediately supply information concerning what the individual must do in order to be saved. On the other hand, if a man or a woman has honest questions, those queries must be dealt with first. Otherwise, there is serious danger that some of the lost will not respond in a whole-souled fashion. Schaeffer maintains, "If they do respond in this way, they have not understood the gospel; they are still lost, and we have defaulted in our task of preaching and communicating the gospel to our generation"[5]

The invitation to act comes only after an adequate foundation of knowledge has been supplied. Conversion does not begin with "accept Christ as Savior," it starts with "good, adequate, and sufficient reasons" to know that Christianity is true. Schaeffer explains:

> *Those who object to the position that there are good, adequate, and sufficient reasons to know with our reason that Christianity is true are left with a probability position at some point. At some point and in some terminology they are left with a leap of faith. . . . Of course, faith is needed to become a Christian, but there are two concepts concerning faith. . . . One idea of faith would be a blind leap in the dark. A blind leap in which you believe something with no reason (or, no adequate reason), you just believe it. . . . The other idea of faith, which has no relationship with this, none whatsoever, is that you are asked to believe something and bow before that something on the basis of good and adequate reasons. . . . The Biblical concept of faith is very much the second and not the first.[6]*

In other words pre-evangelism comes before evangelism — knowledge precedes conversion. *One reason many men and women have not been reached is because Christians have not taken enough time with pre-evangelism.* Often faith in Christ merely awaits a clarification of the truth of Christianity; once this truth is established, honest searchers are anxious to accept Jesus Christ as their Savior. Bill Bright observes, "Most people are not rejecting Christ; for the most part they are rejecting a false impression of Christianity. I find that very few, if any, people who have seriously considered the facts concerning Jesus Christ have said 'no' to him."[7]

Pre-evangelism involves the concept of Christian apologetics, in the sense of *communication* of the faith rather than *defense* of the faith. Although academic study of the defense of the faith can be beneficial to Christians, the primary focus on apologetics should be towards proclaiming the gospel to our generation. In this regard Francis Schaeffer stresses:

> *Apologetics should not be merely an academic subject, a new kind of scholasticism. It should be thought out and practiced in the rough and tumble of living contact with the present generation. Thus, the Christian should not be interested only in presenting a nicely balanced system on its own, like some Greek metaphysical system, but rather in something which has constant contact with reality — the reality of the questions being asked by his own and the next generation.*[8]

The shape of present day Christian communication should be formed out of a detailed look at the problems and questions confronting twentieth century people. Christians *must* face modern intellectual questions such as: Does Christianity conflict with science? Are all religions pathways to God? Does it really matter what a person believes? Why does God allow so much evil and suffering? God's people are obligated to present reasonable answers to such questions, to provide "good, adequate, and sufficient reasons" to know that Christianity is true. Men and women of today *deserve* to know that the Christian view of things makes sense. Clark Pinnock declares that people of this generation "demand to know, and have a *right* to know, that the historical and intellectual foundations beneath the gospel are sound. . . . Our good news is an accredited claim and a bona fide offer."[9]

Christian apologetics, in the sense of *communication* of the faith, "is a putting together of the data common to all Christians in a consistent and scientific whole. It explains why Christians are Christians and why non-Christians should be Christians."[10] C. Stephen Evans notes that it doesn't take a genius to understand that type of information: "If God exists and has provided rational evidence as one way people can know about him, surely it would not require a Ph.D. in philosophy to understand this evidence."[11] Clark Pinnock agrees, "I do not believe we need to commit ourselves without reasonable grounds. I am also convinced the essential reason for the Christian faith can be explained in understandable language."[12]

The real purpose of Christian apologetics is the communication of the faith to our modern generation in understandable terms — the presentation of some sensible and convincing reasons for believing in Christ and accepting him as Lord and Savior. Such dialogue must contain more than just a declaration of the specific contents of the gospel, however. Terry Miethe writes:

> *Scripture shows repeatedly that mere proclamation of the gospel alone did not account for its acceptance. Apostolic witness in Scripture declares again and again the evidential and historical nature of Christianity. Reasoning and argument were used to bring about conversions (Acts 18:4; 9:26-31).*[13]

Although a biblical communication of the faith *includes* gospel content, it also concerns itself with the deepest questions of contemporary man and seeks to satisfactorily answer those questions.

Who is responsible for this communication of faith? H. Eddie Fox and George Morris "see every Christian as a 'called' person who may participate in God's idea of a 'kingdom of priests' — a kingdom of faith-sharers"[14] Insisting that the ministry of Christ was given to the entire congregation, Fox and Morris write:

> *In the New Testament the word* ministry *is never used to denote the responsibility of one select, fully ordained group. The word* ministry *is always used to denote or designate the responsibility of the whole people of God. The clergy are those called of God to serve the laity, that is, to teach them and train them for their life, their work, and especially for their witness and ministry. The ministry of Christ was given to the congregation (Eph. 4:11-13). . . . When the church is gathered, the task of the ordained person relates to the function of word, sacrament, and order. But when the church scatters into the community and the world, there is no real difference in function, responsibility, or accountability for ministry.*[15]

Ephesians 2:13-16 teaches that the church is "one body," one priesthood undifferentiated; all barriers of sex, race, class, and nationality have been abolished. Thus all Christians are called to ministry, and all are ordained by God for service! The Holy Spirit conveyed to the whole people of God power to witness to the saving grace of Jesus Christ. Terry

Miethe asserts, "only when we take the priesthood of all believers seriously can the pastor/teacher be freed up to do the job Scripture says he should do: preparing the saints for the work of ministry so that the body of Christ might be built up" (Eph. 4:11-12).[16]

Other biblical evidence of God's calling of all Christians for service is contained in Matthew's account of the recruitment of Peter, Andrew, James, and John as disciples of Christ. There we note that Jesus did not invite exceptionally bright or well-educated men; those men did not possess academic degrees in the arts of their day, nor did any of them belong to the Levitical priesthood. Instead, our Lord chose ordinary men engaged in fishing, a common occupation in Galilee. "Follow me," Jesus cried to them, "and I will make you fishers of men" (Matt. 4:19).

So it is even today. Being a disciple of Christ does not require exceptional talent or intelligence. What Jesus is looking for are persons who will respond in a positive manner to his invitation to "Follow me." He comes to individuals where they are and invites them to respond to his call. The discipleship to which he summons men and women today is no less than that to which he called those four men — wherever God's children are, whatever their talents, they can spread the Good News of Jesus Christ.

Although the Bible specifically holds all believers responsible for communication of the faith, many Christians ignore their duty to proclaim the gospel, thus relegating the evangelism task to the professional ministers and the fulltime Christian workers. It is tragic that so many believers have turned over the work of evangelism to the so-called "professionals." In my own case, I sincerely believe if someone had been available sooner to help me work through my spiritual questions, I would have become a Christian much earlier. The Christian community desperately needs to understand that the intellectual questions, seen by so many as dry and unimportant, can have a *real* impact on lives — that by failing to answer such questions, they are avoiding a genuine ministry and prolonging the search for God for many people.

The greatest need today is for believers everywhere — in the home, in the work place, in the community and the world, in all walks of life — to testify of God's saving grace. Each child of God should be involved in some way in sharing the gospel message. Of course, such involvement may mean various kinds of ministry for different people, depending on their situations, their abilities, and God's will for them individually. But *each* Christian should participate.

Lay Christians need never downplay their own talents or abilities. In fact, laypersons should be made aware that they are generally *better* equipped than professionals to communicate their faith in terms the non-Christian can readily understand. H. Eddie Fox and George Morris point out, "People will say, 'I am not a good talker.' But, when it comes to the gospel of Jesus Christ there are no 'good talkers.' As a matter of fact, we probably do not want 'slick talkers' trying to represent Jesus Christ. No one can be a glib witness."[17]

A child of God does not have to be "slick talker" to bear a testimony. What the Christian *must* possess is a love for the lost and then the knowledge — biblical and otherwise — to communicate it accurately. *Every believer can learn to do this on an effective level.* Deeply moved by the dire needs of those around them, Fox and Morris write:

> *The heart aches because millions are forced to live unfulfilled lives, victims of poverty, hunger, oppression, and racism. . . . It troubles us deeply to see people in bondage to inner compulsions, such as gluttony, alcoholism, or drug dependency. It hurts to see some of our youth floundering in aimlessness. We are troubled by the decadence of our morally permissive society. In Christ we see the answer to these and other deep personal and societal needs. Thus, we are moved to share the gospel by word and deed.*[18]

It must be clearly emphasized, however, that there are two other essential prerequisites for proclaiming the gospel by word and deed: trust in God and disciplined study. First, believers must be faithful in trusting God as the true source of power for ministry. Calvin Miller points out, "How foolish we are to rebel against God's call to service because we think we can't handle some ministry. We forget that God never asks us to handle it by ourselves. He wants us to develop a dependency on his power."[19] Second, disciples of Christ must be engaged in personal study of the Bible and of good Christian literature. Miller writes, "Consider the relationship of the word *discipline* to the word *disciple*. A key idea in the word *disciple* is that of pupil. Thus the chief discipline of the disciple is study, acquiring knowledge through learning. To be a *disciple* is to be under *discipline*."[20]

Holy Scripture admonishes us to "*study* to shew thyself approved unto

God" (2 Tim. 2:15 KJV), to "grow in grace and *in the knowledge* of our Lord and Saviour Jesus Christ" (2 Peter 3:18 KJV). Yet there are millions of Christians in today's world displaying laziness towards discipleship. Miller comments, "Many disciples would like the happiness that comes from discipline, but they also want to avoid the hard work. Millions of us believers do not take our Christianity seriously simply because discipleship is rigorous and tiring."[21] It is foolish to avoid the life of study, however, simply because it is hard work. Although serious study is demanding, it yields great rewards. Miller elaborates:

> *Only Christians who commit themselves to study and prayer can stand . . . in confidence. It is not always possible to win every one of our battles with the world, but with better spiritual discipline, we position ourselves for victory. Instead of standing naked before Satan, Paul counseled us to put on the whole armor of God (Eph. 6:11). There is a glorious confidence in knowing that we have a sure answer. Having disciplined ourselves we are able to give to everyone who asks a reason — an intelligent reason — for the hope that is in us (1 Peter 3:15).*[22]

Noting that laziness in evangelical matters will never do, Clark Pinnock states, "The total Christian understanding of the world plus the evidences on which that understanding rests form a necessary deposit of knowledge which the Christian needs to master."[23] Scriptural emphasis that knowledge is needed prior to salvation should impel God's people to strive for basic knowledge needed to communicate their faith.

If twentieth century Christians truly care about those around them — if they are really concerned about the men and women, boys and girls searching for answers to contemporary religious questions — they will heed Pinnock's "Evangelical Imperative":

> *The beauty of the gospel is its facticity. But professing it, and demonstrating it publicly are two different things. Conservative Christians have failed to do their homework. . . . The results of this surrender are proving catastrophic. Nothing short of a Christian reformation can alter the direction of the stream. But the change must be brought about. But it will not be done without sweat and tears. Proof texts and slogans will arouse the saints but will not win the battle. If the Christian gospel is to regain a position of authority in shaping the form of our culture, a great deal of hard work is ahead for us.*[24]

Notes

INTRODUCTION

[1]John Warwick Montgomery, *Faith Founded on Fact* (Nashville, TN: Thomas Nelson, 1978), pp. 39-42.

[2]Ibid., p. 42.

[3]Paul Little, *Know Why You Believe* (Wheaton, IL: Victor Books, 1983), p. 147.

[4]Clark Pinnock, *Set Forth Your Case* (Phillipsburg, NJ: Craig Press, 1967), p. 126.

[5]Ibid., p. 9.

[6]John Shelby Spong, *The Easter Moment* (New York, NY: The Seabury Press, 1980). As quoted in George Gallup, Jr. and George O'Connell's *Who Do Americans Say That I Am?* (Louisville, KY: Westminster/John Knox Press, 1986), p. 92. Permission granted by the author.

A PERSONAL GRIEF

[1]Paula D'Arcy, "Song for Sarah," (Wheaton, IL: Harold Shaw, 1979). As condensed from the book in *Reader's Digest*, December 1980, p. 220. Permission granted by the author.

[2]See: Doug Manning, *Don't Take My Grief Away* (San Francisco, CA: Harper and Row, 1984); and Martha Whitmore Hickman, *I Will Not Leave You Desolate* (Nashville, TN: The Upper Room, 1982).

[3]Excerpt from *A Severe Mercy* by Sheldon Vanauken. Copyright©1977, 1980 by Sheldon Vanauken. Reprinted by permission of HarperCollins Publishers.

[4]Chad Walsh, "Afterword," *A Grief Observed* (New York, NY: The Seabury Press, 1976), p. 113.

A REASONABLE FAITH

CHAPTER ONE

[1]Robert Dean, *How Can We Believe?* (Nashville, TN: Broadman Press, 1978), p. 15. Permission granted by the author, who holds the copyright.

[2]John Warwick Montgomery, *History and Christianity* (Minneapolis, MN: Bethany House, 1972), pp. 15-16.

[3]Stephen Board, "Fact and Faith in Modern Theology," *Christianity Today*, 26 May 1967, pp. 7-8.

[4]Clark Pinnock, *Reason Enough* (Downers Grove, IL: Inter-Varsity Press, 1980), p. 74.

[5]See: Jim Denton and Jon Trott, "Kierkegaard: The Existential Christian," *Cornerstone* Vol. 17, Issue 88 (1989), pp. 23-24.

[6]Maurene Fell Pierson, "The Heresy of Simple Faith," *Theology Today*, October 1963, pp. 339-340.

[7]Little, *Know Why You Believe*, p. 11.

[8]From UNDECEPTIONS by C.S. Lewis Copyright©1970 by C.S. Lewis Pte Ltd, reproduced by permission of Curtis Brown Ltd, London.

[9]Charles Swindoll, *Growing Deep in the Christian Life* (Portland, OR: Multomah Press, 1986), p. 27.

[10]Elton Trueblood, "Rational Christianity," *Christianity Today*, 14 February 1969, p. 3.

[11]*Ibid.*, p. 5.

[12]Jeff Amano, "Cults Fed by Churches that Fail to Feed the Intellect," *Word and Way*, 18 September 1986, p. 12.

[13]*Ibid.*

[14]Gallup, Jr. and O'Connell, *Who Do American Say That I Am?*, pp. 68-69.

[15]*Ibid.*, p. 69.

[16]See Gene Edward Veith, Jr.'s excellent book *Loving God With All Your Mind* (Westchester, IL: Crossway Books, 1987), especially pp. 143-149.

[17]Pinnock, *Reason Enough*, p. 13.

CHAPTER TWO

[1]Lloyd Ogilve, *Ask Him Anything* (Dallas, TX: WORD Incorporated, 1981), p. 9.

[2]Alan Richardson, *Christian Apologetics* (New York, NY: Harper and Row, 1947), p. 22. Reprinted by permission of SCM Press, London, England.

[3]Pierson, "The Heresy of Simple Faith," p. 342.

[4]Edward John Carnell, *Christian Commitment* (New York, NY: Macmillan, 1957), p. 142.

[5]*Ibid.*, pp. 82-83.

[6]Jay Kesler, *Breakthrough* (Wheaton, IL: Campus Life Books, 1981), p. 24.

[7]J. B. Phillips, *Your God is Too Small* (New York, NY: Macmillan, 1961), p. 8. Additional rights granted by Epworth Press, Cambridge, England.

[8]Colin Chapman, *The Case for Christianity* (Grand Rapids, MI: Eerdmans, 1981), p. 123.

[9]C.S.Lewis, *The Weight of Glory and Other Addresses* (New York, NY: Macmillan, 1980), p. 28. Reprinted by permission of HarperCollins, London, England.

[10]Josh McDowell, *Answers to Tough Questions* (San Bernardino, CA: Here's Life, 1983), p. 119.

[11]Terry Miethe, *A Christian's Guide to Faith and Reason* (Minneapolis, MN: Bethany House, 1987), p. 29.

[12]Carnell, *Christian Commitment*, p. 198.

CHAPTER THREE

[1]Lewis Carroll, *Alice's Adventure in Wonderland and Through the Looking Glass* (New York, NY: Parents Magazine Press, 1964), pp. 71-72.

[2]McDowell, *Answers to Tough Questions*, pp. 149-150.

[3]C. E. M. Joad, "The Plight of the Intellectual," *The Fate of Man* (New York, NY: George Braziller, 1961), p. 367.

[4]M. Vernon Davis, "Christianity Needs Performance, Not Defense," *Word and Way,* 12 November 1987, p. 11.

[5]Miethe, *A Christian's Guide to Faith and Reason,* p. 114.

[6]Calvin Miller, *A Hunger for Meaning* (Downers Grove, IL: Inter-Varsity Press, 1984), p. 12.

[7]Taken from the book, THE INTELLECT AND BEYOND by Oliver Barclay, Copyright©1985 by the Zondervan Corporation. Used by permission.

[8]Francis Schaeffer, *The Complete Works of Francis A. Schaeffer,* Volume I (Westchester, IL: Crossway Books, 1982), p. 154.

[9]Miethe, *A Christian's Guide to Faith and Reason,* pp. 17-18.

[10]F. R. Beattie, *Apologetics* (Richmond, VA: Presbyterian Committee of Publication, 1903), pp. 37-38.

[11]Miethe, *A Christian's Guide to Faith and Reason,* p. 120.

[12]Excerpt from *Faith and Reason* by Nels F.S. Ferre. Copyright 1946 by Harper and Brothers Publishers, Inc., copyright renewed, 1974 by Mrs. Nels F.S. Ferre. Reprinted by permission of HarperCollins Publishers.

[13]Little, *Know Why You Believe,* p. 142.

[14]Richard Dugan, *How to Know You'll Live Forever* (Minneapolis, MN: Bethany House, 1984), p. 133.

[15]Carnell, *Christian Commitment,* pp. 76-77.

CHAPTER FOUR

[1]Kenneth Boa and Larry Moody, *I'm Glad You Asked* (Wheaton, IL: Victor Books, 1982), p. 64.

[2]Lewis Drummond and Paul Baxter, *How to Respond to a Skeptic* (Chicago, IL: Moody Press, 1986), p. 23.

[3]Pinnock, *Reason Enough,* p. 34.

[4]*Ibid.*

[5]*Ibid.,* p. 35.

[6]Swindoll, *Growing Deep in the Christian Life,* pp. 54-55.

[7]Little, *Know Why You Believe,* pp. 148-149.

[8]Harry Blamines, *On Christian Truth* (Ann Arbor, MI: Servant Publications, 1983), pp. 7-8.

[9]Ferre, *Faith and Reason,* p. 193.

[10]From the book *Questions Non-Christians Ask* by Barry Wood, Copyright©1977 by Fleming H. Revell. Used by permission of Fleming H. Revell Company.

[11]See: Terry Miethe (ed.), Gary Habermas, and Antony G. N. Flew, *Did Jesus Rise From the Dead? The Resurrection Debate* (San Francisco, CA: Harper and Row, 1987).

[12]Josh McDowell, *Evidence That Demands a Verdict* (San Bernardino, CA: Here's Life, 1979), p. 327.

CHAPTER FIVE

[1]Little, *Know Why You Believe,* p. 139.

[2]Cliffe Knechtle, *Give Me an Answer* (Downers Grove, IL: Inter-Varsity Press, 1986), p. 19.

[3]C. S. Lewis, *Mere Christianity* (New York, NY: Macmillan, 1952), p. 43. Reprinted by permission of HarperCollins, London, England.

[4]See books like: George Eldon Ladd, *I Believe in the Resurrection of Jesus* (Eerdmans, 1975); Michael Green, *The Empty Cross of Jesus* (Inter-Varsity Press, 1984); John Wenham, *Easter Enigma: Are the Resurrection Accounts in Conflict?* (Zondervan, 1984); Frank Morrison, *Who Moved the Stone* (Zondervan, 1958); and Terry Miethe (ed.), Gary Habermas, and Antony G. N. Flew, *Did Jesus Rise From the Dead? The Resurrection Debate* (Harper and Row, 1989) has an excellent bibliography.

[5]McDowell, *Answers to Tough Question,* p. 64.

[6]Lewis, *Mere Christianity,* p. 65.

[7]Taken from the book, REASON TO BELIEVE by R.C. Sproul, Copyright©1981 by R.C. Sproul. Used by permission of Zondervan Publishing House.

[8]Little, *Know Why You Believe,* p. 131.

CHAPTER SIX

[1]There is a *growing* body of literature from both sides regarding this "conflict." The following books are valuable: Donald Mackay, *Science and the Quest for Meaning* (Eerdmans, 1982); Charles Hummel, *The Galileo Connection: Resolving Conflicts between Science and the Bible* (Inter-Varsity, 1986); Robert Gange, *Origins and Destiny: A Scientist Examines God's Handiwork* (Word Books, 1986); A. E. Wilder Smith, *Man's Origin, Man's Destiny* (Bethany House Publishers, 1968); Norman Macbeth, *Darwin Retried: An Appeal to Reason* (Gambit, 1971); Charles Thaxton, Walter Bradley, and Roger Olsen, *The Mystery of Life's Origin: Reassessing Current Theories* (Philosophical Library, 1984); and Henry Morris and Gary Parker, *What is Creation Science?* (Creation-Life Publishers, Inc., 1982).

[2]But not all Christian Scholars hold to a "young earth" theory; see Davis Young, *Christianity and the Age of the Earth* (Eerdmans, 1982).

[3]Don Stewart, *99 Questions People Ask Most About the Bible* (Wheaton, IL: Tyndale House, 1982), p. 107.

[4]*Ibid.,* p. 100.

[5]For the best statement of just what biblical inerrancy does entail see "The Chicago Statement on Biblical Inerrancy," pp. 493-502 in *Inerrancy,* edited by Norman L. Geisler (Zondervan, 1979).

[6]Reprinted by permission by Macmillan Publishing Company from *Is God a Creationist?* edited by Roland Mushat Frye. Copyright©1983 by Charles Scribner's Sons.

[7]Davis Young, "Christianity and the Age of the Earth," in *Is God a Creationist?,* p. 84.

[8]Edwin Olson, "Hidden Agenda Behind the Evolution/Creationist Debate," in *Is God a Creationist?,* p. 40.

[9]Young, "Christianity and the Age of the Earth," pp. 92-93.

[10]*Ibid.,* p. 86.

[11]Langdon Gilkey, "Creationism: The Roots of the Conflict," in *Is God A Creationist?,* p. 64.

[12]Dean, *How Can We Believe?*, p. 20. Permission granted by the author, who holds the copyright.

[13]Michael Green, *Faith for the Non-Religious* (Wheaton, IL: Tyndale House, 1979), pp. 37-39.

[14]David Field and Peter Toon, *Real Questions* (Batavia, IL and Herts, England: Lion, 1984), p. 85.

[15]Wilbur Garrett, "Where Did We Come From?", *National Geographic,* October 1988, p. 434.

[16]John Putman, "The Search for Modern Humans," *National Geographic,* October 1988, p. 460.

[17]Jack Wood Sears, *Conflict and Harmony in Science and the Bible* (Grand Rapids, MI: Baker Book House, 1969), p. 13.

[18]Young, "Christianity and the Age of the Earth," p. 88.

CHAPTER SEVEN

[1]McDowell, *Answers to Tough Questions,* p. 39.

[2]See: Jon Buell and O. Quentin Hyder, *Jesus: God, Ghost, or Guru?* (Zondervan, 1978).

[3]Lewis, *Mere Christianity,* pp. 55-56.

[4]C. S. Lewis, *Miracles* (New York, NY: Macmillan, 1960), p. 109. Reprinted by permission of HarperCollins, London, England.

[5]From: *More Than a Carpenter.* By: Josh McDowell©1977. Used by permission of Tyndale House Publishers, Inc. All Rights Reserved.

[6]Philip Schaff, *The Person of Christ* (New York, NY: American Tract Society, 1913), pp. 94-95, 97.

[7]John R. W. Stott, *Basic Christianity* (Grand Rapids, MI: Eerdmans, 1983), p. 40.

[8]Lewis Sperry Chafer, *Systematic Theology* (Dallas, TX: Dallas Theological Seminary Press, 1947), p. 21.

[9]See: Miethe, Habermas, Flew, *Did Jesus Rise From the Dead? The Resurrection Debate* (Harper and Row, 1989).

[10]Michael Green, *Man Alive* (Downers Grove, IL: Inter-Varsity Press, 1968), p. 54.

CHAPTER EIGHT

[1]See: Terry Miethe, *The New Christian's Guide to Following Jesus* (Minneapolis, MN: Bethany House, 1984). His excellent chapter on "The Problem of Evil" contains a full discussion of the Augustine solution.

[2]Excerpt from *Philosophy of Religion* by Elton Trueblood. Copyright©1957 by Elton Trueblood. Reprinted by permission of HarperCollins Publishers.

[3]C. S. Lewis, *The Problem of Pain* (New York, NY: Macmillan, 1962), p. 26. Reprinted by permission of Harper Collins, London, England.

[4]*Ibid.,* pp. 33-34.

[5]Dean, *How Can We Believe?,* pp. 37-38. Permission granted by the author, who holds the copyright.

[6]Pat Robertson, *Answers To 200 Of Life's Most Probing Questions* (Nashville, TN: Thomas Nelson Publishers, 1984), p. 20.

[7]Lewis, *The Problem of Pain,* p. 40.

[8]John Allan and Gus Eyre, *A Field Guide to Christianity* (Chicago, IL: Moody Press, 1986), p. 161. Reprinted by permission of Paternoster Press, Exeter, England.

[9]Drummond and Baxter, *How to Respond to a Skeptic,* p. 42.

[10]Lewis, *The Problem of Pain,* p. 93.

[11]Billy Graham, *Facing Death and the Life After* (Dallas, TX: WORD Incorporated 1987), p. 90.

[12]Field and Toon, *Real Questions,* p. 89.

[13]Knechtle, *Give Me An Answer,* p. 56.

[14]Little, *Know Why You Believe,* pp. 127-128.

CHAPTER NINE

[1]McDowell, *Answers to Tough Questions,* p. 2.

[2]Paul Little, *Know What You Believe* (Wheaton, IL: Victor Books, 1984), p. 10.

[3]Stewart, *99 Questions People Ask Most About the Bible,* p. 90.

[4]Taken from: *Answering the Tough Ones* by David Dewitt. Copyright 1980. Moody Bible Institute of Chicago. Moody Press. Used by permission.

[5]See: F. F Bruce, *Are the New Testament Documents Reliable?* (Eerdmans, 1960); and John A. T. Robinson, *Can We Trust the New Testament?* (Eerdmans, 1977).

[6]Montgomery, *History and Christianity,* p. 29.

[7]Fenton Hort and Brooke Westcott, *The New Testament in the Original Greek* (New York, NY: Macmillan, 1881), Vol. 1, p. 561.

[8]Stewart, *99 Questions People Ask Most About the Bible,* p. 71.

[9]See: Gary Habermas, *The Verdict of History: Conclusive Evidence for the Life of Jesus* (Nashville, TN: Thomas Nelson, 1988).

[10]Wood, *Questions Non-Christians Ask,* p. 18.

[11]McDowell, *Answers to Tough Questions,* p. 75.

[12]Billy Graham, *Peace With God* (Dallas, TX: WORD BOOKS, 1984), pp. 24-25.

CHAPTER TEN

[1]Harold Bryson, *The Reality of Hell and the Goodness of God* (Wheaton, IL: Tyndale House, 1984), pp. 86-87.

[2]"Evangelism not SBC Priority, Charges HMB's Banks," *Word and Way,* 11 August 1988, p. 12.

[3]William Spurrier, *Guide to the Christian Faith* (New York, NY: Charles Scribner's Sons, 1952), pp. 163-164.

[4]Pinnock, *Reason Enough,* p. 110.

[5]Dewitt, *Answering the Tough Ones,* pp. 65-66.

[6]Wood, *Questions Non-Christians Ask,* p. 100.

[7]Dewitt, *Answering the Tough Ones,* p. 67.

[8]Wood, *Questions Non-Christians Ask,* p. 107.

CHAPTER ELEVEN

[1]Sproul, *Reason to Believe,* p. 77.

[2]Graham, *Peace With God,* p. 181.

[3]Wood, *Questions Non-Christians Ask,* p. 51.

[4]Boa and Moody, *I'm Glad You Asked,* p. 166.

[5]Allan and Eyre, *A Field Guide to Christianity,* p. 85.

[6]Little, *Know What You Believe,* p. 136.

[7]Graham, *Peace With God,* pp. 180-181.

[8]Robertson, *Answers to 200 of Life's Most Probing Questions,* p. 128.

[9]Swindoll, *Growing Deep in the Christian Life,* p. 362.

[10]Allan and Eyre, *A Field Guide to Christianity,* pp. 97-98.

[11]Woods, *Questions Non-Christians Ask,* p. 52.

[12]Philip Yancy and Tim Stafford, *Secrets of the Christian Life* (Wheaton, IL: Campus Life Books, 1979), p. 152.

CHAPTER TWELVE

[1]Schaeffer, *The Complete Works of Francis A. Schaeffer,* Volume I, p. 177.

[2]*Ibid.,* p. 279.

[3]See: Terry L. Miethe's *A Christian's Guide to Faith and Reason* (Bethany House, 1987), especially *Appendix B* "A Plea for the Practical Application of Christian Philosophy," pp. 112-122.

[4]Schaeffer, *The Complete Works of Francis A. Schaeffer,* Volume I, pp. 139-140.

[5]*Ibid.,* p. 196.

[6]*Ibid.,* pp. 181-182.

[7]This portion is taken from "Decision" magazine, November, 1987; ©1987 Billy Graham Evangelistic Association. Used by permission. All rights reserved.

[8]Schaeffer, *The Complete Works of Francis A. Schaeffer,* Volume I, pp. 152-153.

[9]Pinnock, *Set Forth Your Case,* p. 7.

[10]Taken from the book, CLASSICAL APOLOGETICS by R. C. Sproul, John Gerstner, and Arthur W. Lindsley, Copyright©1984 by the Zondervan Corporation. Used by permission.

[11]·C. Stephen Evans, *The Quest for Faith* (Downers Grove, IL: Inter-Varsity Press, 1986), p. 25.

[12]Pinnock, *Reason Enough,* p. 7.

[13]Miethe, *A Christian's Guide to Faith and Reason,* pp. 64-65.

[14]Taken from the book, FAITH SHARING, A Wesleyan View of our Spiritual Journey, by H. Eddie Fox and George E. Morris. Copyright©1986 by the World Methodist Council published by Discipleship Resources.

[15]*Ibid.,* p. 71.

[16]Miethe, *A Christian's Guide to Faith and Reason,* pp. 36-37.

[17]Fox and Morris, *Faith-Sharing,* p. 75.

[18]*Ibid.,* p. 20.

[19]Calvin Miller, *The Taste of Joy* (Downers Grove, IL: Inter-Varsity Press, 1983), p. 137.

[20]*Ibid.,* pp. 17-18.

[21]*Ibid.,* p. 18.

[22]Miller, *A Hunger for Meaning,* p. 53.

[23]Pinnock, *Set Forth Your Case,* p. 18.

[24]*Ibid.,* p. 128.

Suggestions for Further Reading

Barclay, Oliver. *The Intellect and Beyond: Developing a Christian Mind.* Grand Rapids, MI: Zondervan, 1985.

Blamires, Harry. *The Christian Mind.* London: S.P.C.K., 1963.

Carnell, Edward John. *Christian Commitment.* New York, NY: Macmillan, 1957.

Evans, C. Stephen. *The Quest for Faith.* Downers Grove, IL: Inter-Varsity Press, 1986.

Fox, H. Eddie and George E. Morris. *Faith-Sharing.* Grand Rapids, MI: Francis Asbury Press, 1986.

Gallup, Jr., George and George O'Connell. *Who Do Americans Say That I Am?* Philadelphia, PA: Westminister Press, 1986.

Green, Michael. *Runaway World.* Downers Grove, IL: Inter-Varsity Press, 1968.

Lewis, C. S. *The Case for Christianity.* New York, NY: Macmillan, 1956.

————. *Mere Christianity.* New York, NY: Macmillan, 1960.

————. *Miracles: How God Intervenes in Nature and Human Affairs.* New York, NY: Macmillan, 1960.

————. *The Problem of Pain: The Intellectual Problem Raised by Human Suffering, Examined With Sympathy and Realism.* New York, NY: Macmillan, 1962.

Little, Paul. *Know Why You Believe.* Wheaton, IL: Victor Books, 1983.

————. *Know What You Believe.* Wheaton, IL: Victor Books, 1984.

Miethe, Terry. *A Christian's Guide to Faith and Reason.* Minneapolis, MN: Bethany House, 1987.

————. *The New Christian's Guide to Following Jesus.* Minneapolis, MN: Bethany House, 1984.

Miller, Calvin. *A Hunger for Meaning.* Downers Grove, IL: Inter-Varsity Press, 1984.

Montgomery, John Warwick. *Faith Founded on Fact*. Nashville, TN: Thomas Nelson, 1978.

————. *History and Christianity*. Minneapolis, MN: Bethany House, 1972.

Pinnock, Clark. *Reason Enough*. Downers Grove, IL: Inter-Varsity Press, 1980.

————. *Set Forth Your Case*. Phillipsburg, NJ: Craig Press, 1967.

Purtill, Richard. *C. S. Lewis's Case for the Christian Faith*. San Francisco, CA: Harper and Row, 1985.

Schaeffer, Francis. *The Complete Works of Francis A. Schaeffer, Volume I*. Westchester, IL: Crossway Books, 1982.

Sproul, R. C., John Gerstner, and Authur W. Lindsley. *Classical Apologetics*. Grand Rapids, MI: Zondervan, 1984.

Stott, John R. W. *Your Mind Matters: The Place of the Mind in the Christian Life*. Downers Grove, IL: Inter-Varsity Press, 1972.

Veith, Gene Edward, Jr. *Loving God With All Your Mind*. Westchester, IL: Crossway Books, 1987.